PRAISE FOR
CREATING SALES STARS

"Schiffman and Krebs do a masterful job of turning timeless principles into specific tools to enable salespeople to sell. Treat people with respect, listen, show empathy, personalize relationships, communicate, and make others better—all are translated into proven techniques that will create sales stars. Wonderful ideas not just for Millennials and salespeople, but for all of us wanting to make a difference."

—DAVE ULRICH,
Rensis Likert professor, Ross School of Business,
University of Michigan; partner, The RBL Group;
and author of *Victory Through Organization* and *The Why of Work*

"Stephan Schiffman's legendary and iconic sales training and coaching strategies have been instrumental in supporting my own sales and leadership growth and success for the past twenty-five years. In his latest timely book, *Creating Sales Stars*, he has transcended his earlier trainings into meeting the critical needs of today's generation. This book offers simple steps and techniques to ignite your sales team to be successful performers. Thank you, Steve, for giving us another GEM!"

—DONNA TERJESEN,
managing director, HBR Consulting

"Millennials are the most powerful influencers to enter the twenty-first-century workforce. Their ability to challenge and be challenged has been defined in Stephan Schiffman and Gary Krebs's well-thought-out book, *Creating Sales Stars*. Truly a powerful generation with ambition and drive for results!"

—MITCH PODOB,
vice president, Global Human Resources, Timex Group

"Stephan Schiffman is always focused on results and the steps needed to achieve them. We operate in very competitive markets, and his ideas, insights, and techniques are both ageless and dynamic. This book is sure to help you adapt to a new and ever-changing world."

—BOB JOHNSON,
CEO and founder, Kaffe Magnum Opus

"Schiffman gives you the tools you need to break through to the Millennials in your organization, who do have a different mindset from past generations. Schiffman's clear and concise guidance in *Creating Sales Stars* provides the answer on how to get this group of people to thrive in your organization."

—JOSH SANDERS,
vice president, Sea Breeze

"Schiffman's book unlocks the secrets for managing the new sales force. He provides the steps needed to achieve positive results from any sales team—especially the incoming generation."

—J. PETER BENET,
CFP®, CLU, owner, Benet Financial Services

"Stephan Schiffman's books and training are often watershed moments for sales teams and their leaders. I have witnessed the results of Stephan's teachings firsthand and watched them move the sales needle upward almost immediately. Many of my past employees comment to me that his books and training continue to have an impact on their sales careers and their lives. This book surpasses Schiffman's prior works in terms of relevance and timeliness, and will no doubt also become a watershed moment for generations of sales professionals and leaders to come."

—DAN STARR,
vice president of sales channel development, pdvWireless

"Steve Schiffman has done it again! In his most important book since *Ask Questions, Get Sales*, he has delivered a hands-on, street-level instruction that bridges the gap between past-gen and new-gen salespeople. Steve and Gary Krebs's compelling and useful approach to managing this new era of sales professionals will deliver positive results and take your sales team to the highest level. *Creating Sales Stars* is a must read for business leaders, sales managers . . . and, yes, even millennials."

—STEPHEN MUELLER,
managing director, OneBeacon Insurance

"Nothing happens in a company until someone sells something. You might offer the best product or service in the world, but if your sales team is stuck and not closing deals, your organization won't go anywhere. The twenty-five principles in this book will supercharge your team to make sales—and help you become a better leader too. From implementing the right training to creating a fun and interactive work environment to communicating in a manner that translates to employees of all generations, *Creating Sales Stars* is the one book you need to retain your best people and get them fired up to make sales while maintaining your own sanity."

—RICHARD O. WARTHER,
founder, president, and CEO, Vanguard ID Systems, Inc.

CREATING
SALES
STARS

CREATING SALES STARS

A GUIDE TO MANAGING THE MILLENNIALS ON YOUR TEAM

STEPHAN SCHIFFMAN

Bestselling Author of *Cold Calling Techniques* and
25 Habits of Highly Successful Salespeople

• WITH GARY M. KREBS •

HarperCollins
LEADERSHIP
AN IMPRINT OF HarperCollins

Published by HarperCollins Leadership, an imprint of HarperCollins.

Book design by Elyse Strongin, Neuwirth & Associates.

978-0-8144-3940-1 (eBook)

Library of Congress Control Number: 2018954570

978-0-8144-3938-8

Printed in the United States of America
18 19 20 21 22 LSC 10 9 8 7 6 5 4 3 2 1

*Dedicated to Sales Leaders everywhere—who suffer
a lot more than people realize*

ACKNOWLEDGMENTS

Whenever one takes on a project like this, there are numerous people who should be thanked for their efforts. First, with deep appreciation, I'd like to thank my agent and friend, Gary M. Krebs. It was Gary who persuaded me to write this book in the first place, and I am grateful for his steadfast help and guidance. I don't think this book could have been done without him.

I am deeply indebted to all our clients, as well as the myriad business leaders, salespeople, and HR professionals who offered their wisdom in helping create this work.

The folks at HarperCollins Leadership and the former AMACOM have been exceptional to work with. I am especially proud to be working with an editor as exceptional, enthusiastic, and responsive as Timothy Burgard. I would also like to acknowledge Ellen R. Kadin, who originally received the proposal and passed it along to Tim for acquisition. The talented folks at Neuwirth & Associates—Phil Gaskill, Jeff Farr, and Beth Metrick—did an excellent job copyediting and seeing the book through production.

I have had the good fortune of having written and published 72 books over the years. It has taken a lot of patience and persistence from others to enable me to accomplish that. Anne, my wife and partner, has been with me every step of the way. I do not know how far I would have gotten if it hadn't been for her. She never stopped believing in the story that I told her when we first met—how I planned to speak, write, and travel throughout the world. This has all come to pass and we are still together.

My two children, Daniel and Jennifer, now have their own beautiful children: Justin, Julia, Dylan, Jordan, and Zoe. Thank you, with all my love.

Gary would like to offer his special thanks to Evan Krebs, a natural-born salesperson if ever there was one, who provided inspiration along the way. On the HR front, Mitch Podub has been a source of never-ending support and wisdom. Also thanks to Bill Gladstone, Peter McGuigan, John Willig, Grace Freedson, Alan Axelrod, Rick Frishman, Anne Alexander, Michael DeMartin, Mark Donenfeld, and Sheila Buff, without whom GMK Writing and Editing, Inc. would never have materialized.

And, of course, Gary sends his personal love and gratitude to Liz, Justin, and Ilana for putting up with his oddball writing quirks and Pearl Jam turned up to eleven.

CONTENTS

FOREWORD

A word doesn't define who I am.

The above quote seems to be the rallying cry for almost everyone, but it's especially true for the Millennial generation.

Millennials, those aged 18–34, are currently America's largest generation, surpassing Baby Boomers. Millennials have acquired somewhat of a reputation in some circles. They have been described as selfish, disengaged, and disconnected from other forms of human contact, because they prefer to communicate through technology. On the positive side, they're tech savvy and tend to favor brands and companies with a strong corporate social responsibility program, and they love to collaborate with their colleagues.

But—are these descriptions accurate?

It depends on whom you ask. One thing we know for sure if this: no one group is a monolith. People who box an entire generation into one category are making a huge mistake—especially if you're in sales or marketing. Those so-called "experts" are doing a disservice to their brand, their company, and to an entire generation.

Millennials can be extremely beneficial to any organization. They're capable of breathing new life into every day routines, seeing things from a different—sometimes fresher—perspective, and injecting a youthful exuberance that can give an organization a much needed boost. Managers need to understand that this generation absorbs things differently than previous generations.

My motto is "adapt, change, or die." If you, as a manager, are making your Millennials conform to the norm of "how things used to be" or "because that's how it's always been," you might as well get out of business.

This book addresses a real concern many companies and managers are having all over the world: collaborating with, motivating, and managing the next generation of sales rock stars poised to take your company to the next level.

Let go of complacency and learn to speak their language.

—Jeffrey Hayzlett,
primetime TV & radio host, speaker, author,
and part-time cowboy

CREATING
SALES
STARS

•
•
•

OLD-SCHOOL MANAGEMENT DOESN'T WORK!

Since you have purchased this book and are now holding it in your hands, I assume it means you have arrived at an important conclusion about today's emerging sales professionals: they are a puzzle!

Unlike salespeople from the past, they don't visibly seem to have the self-motivation and fire in the belly to try to break sales records. These past few years, I've been consulting with companies of all different sizes and types of industries and have found that they are all struggling to figure out these critical issues with their sales teams:

- How to keep them focused on sales
- How to find and hire the right young people
- How to motivate them to beat targets
- How to retain the good ones
- How to train them to get to the next level and create *sales stars*

Do any of the above challenges sound familiar to you?

I'm hearing over and over again from sales leaders that new employees today start out with the same unrealistic expectations. They come out of college thinking they're going to work for Microsoft or Google and make $100K right off the bat. They don't like to intern and don't get the idea of "paying dues" while working to climb up a career ladder. They share and compare their salaries not only with friends and family members in different types of businesses, but with all the other salespeople (and a few non-salespeople, too) in the company. They don't seem to understand or appreciate that some of the salespeople are making bigger bucks because a) they have many more years of experience, b) they have far more contacts and relationships, c) they have extensive institutional and industry knowledge, and d) their sales results are *higher*.

A dangerous phenomenon has been occurring over the years. Sales organizations don't have what I refer to as a "*back bench*" of upcoming, experienced sales stars and potential sales managers to rise up and fill future openings. Managers are in a bind because they have no one to replace retiring salespeople who have all the skills and experience and know the customers, the products, and the markets. Thus, the sales team's back bench either is weak or has a gap as wide as the Grand Canyon.

What's the underlying issue here? *Turnover.*

A recent Gallup poll showed clear-cut evidence that the new workforce thrives on "job-hopping," going from one gig to the next. They don't seem to care one iota about company dedication or what all this job-changing looks like on their résumés, which actually used to matter (and, seemingly, no longer does).

In the old days—I won't date myself by saying what that might be, but it's not as far back as you might think—salespeople wanted to stay in companies to expand their territories, widen their client bases, develop product and industry expertise, move up the ladder, build the 401K, enter management, and so on. Going back a decade (or two or three or four . . .), sales professionals wanted to remain in companies and retire gracefully from them (or die, whichever came first). A fabulous company party would be held in honor of their many years of dedicated service. There'd be a cake and balloons—and maybe even a gold watch inside a fancy gift box.

"*For he's a jolly good fellow, for he's a jolly good fellow, for he's a jolly good fellow—which nobody can deny,*" the entire staff would sing.

The boss proclaims in grand fashion: "Thank you for all your years of dedicated service, Mr. Parker. Here's a one-of-a-kind desk plaque."

Today's generation that recently entered the workforce does not have the same long-term commitment to the company as past employees did. They are impatient with achieving career goals and are cavalier about job-hopping. According to Gallup, one fifth of employees born between 1980 and 1996 changes jobs each year, which is three times greater than other age groups. Six out of every ten people in this same age group are actively looking to change jobs. This probably means that on your team, you have maybe one or two people at most—if that many—who aren't thinking about leaving or actively trying to do so.

Holy Moses—that's a lot of hours you've wasted on-boarding, training, coaching, and mentoring these folks. Gallup estimates the cost of all this turnover is in the neighborhood of $30.5 billion each year!

What, exactly, is going on here? These young professionals have seen their parents laid off from companies during the recession between December 2007 and February 2010 and are well aware of documented corporate corruption (especially in banking). They have no qualms about leaving a company shortly after starting, which means managers struggle to find people to groom who have the staying power to become players—i.e., back-bench players. Certainly, no one lasts long enough to become a bona fide *star*.

If you were drawn to this book, constant turnover is likely only the tip of the iceberg of the problems you are facing. Maybe your sales team needs incessant prodding to pound the pavement and make sales. Or, they are waiting forever for the rest of the team to weigh in on the exact right sales approach to take before hitting the road to meet a customer. Or, perhaps they are e-mailing and texting so much, they forgot that their customers might actually want a personal call every once in a while to know that a living, breathing person is paying attention to them and has their back.

Today's sales force isn't unknowledgeable, lazy, or uncaring, although sometimes it might seem that way. In fact, as you will discover, in some respects the incoming sales class may be *more knowledgeable, more active, and more caring* than the generations preceding them. They are just wildly different. The requisite skill sets need to be creatively teased out of them in order for you to get the results you need and convince them to commit to you for the long haul.

How are they different? They are—dare I use the dirty word—*Millennials*. And with that moniker comes a host of issues you never expected you would have to face as a sales leader—and certainly were never trained or prepared for.

Who Are Millennials?

Millennials are people born between the years 1982 and 1993. There are over 56 million of them in the workplace, which means that as long ago as 2016 they succeeded the Gen-Xers as the largest percentage of the workforce. By the turn of the next decade, they will constitute *50% of the employment population.* This means that, if you run a sales organization, you'd better figure out how to lead and motivate these individuals—*fast.*

Millennials are not only growing in numbers, they are also the most culturally diverse group in the United States. Their worldviews were shaped during turbulent political and economic times and included 9/11, the Great Recession, and some pretty far-out and ugly presidential campaigns and political turmoil. At the same time, they grew up in an age of remarkable technological advancements and new perspectives on globalization and the environment, among other areas.

These twenty- and thirty-somethings have unique belief systems and have even developed their own generational vocabulary that baffles Boomers and Gen-Xers. This group poses an entirely new set of challenges for sales managers accustomed to directing Boomers and Gen-Xers and, as a result, avoidable mistakes abound.

Let's come back to the issue I addressed earlier. Many sales managers regard their Millennial team members as *lazy, spoiled, and spoon-fed.* But is this perception myth, or fact?

The answer is somewhere in the middle. Supervisors and managers are frustrated because they don't understand that Millennials view the world—especially work—differently. In particular, sales managers accustomed to "old-school" approaches need to understand the unique perspectives of Millennials and adapt to them with a whole new style guide on how to lead, inspire, direct, and motivate them. That's where this book comes in.

The First Thing to Know: Don't Use the Word *Millennial*

Many, though not all, Millennials dislike their moniker, feeling it is somehow derogatory and/or presumes certain classifications and attributes that, more often than not, describe them unfavorably.

Fine. Don't use it—you don't need to. The worst thing to do is to have a 1:1 with an employee and say "You have some lazy tendencies—but I forgive you because you're a Millennial."

These folks have been known to be more sensitive to such language (there I go again with labels like "sensitive"!) and would be especially offended by the suggestion that somehow laziness is representative of an entire grouping. They might go as far as equating it to a racial or sexist slur.

The truth of the matter is that what you would view as "lazy"—such as an employee who comes in late or is hardly at her desk—can be something else entirely. Your youthful staff—which grew up in the heyday of the cultural takeover of the Internet, phone devices, and social media—is accustomed to "working" at oddball hours that you don't see. They could be checking work-related e-mails at any hour of the day—before breakfast, during the commute, at dinner with their parents, or at three in the morning—and *consider that work*. By our standards, Millennials conflate work and play; they are interchangeable and you can't judge them for this.

Think of it this way: When you received your first cell phone, the device was probably acquired, programmed, and paid for by your company. The first laptop you received was strictly for work. Just a scant few years later, you bought your own iPhone—probably used for *both* work e-mail and personal use (unless you are a politician!)—and a separate laptop or iPad for home use.

Meanwhile, at the same time that you were getting all of your Steve Jobs-produced tech goodies, so were all these Millennials. The differences in usage were nothing short of astounding: not only were the younger folks more adept at figuring out these devices, they were finding hidden tricks and extras on them and learning to communicate in newly invented vocabularies that only they and their friends could understand.

E-mailing, while used by them as needed, was for the *old folks*. They were texting, using emojis, signing up in chat rooms—and, most of all, *gaming*. Ask anyone under thirty their favorite games, and they will probably name a hundred in under a minute that you've never heard of. In those same sixty seconds, you would probably struggle to come up with maybe three—Words with Friends, Angry Birds, and Pac-Man.

Distinguishing between cultural patterns and tendencies on the one hand and a genuinely under-performing employee on the other can be a daunting task for any manager. So, how do you determine whether your frustration and the employee's shortcomings are the result of poor performance or your lack of understanding of how to properly train, manage, and communicate with her?

That is exactly where I can be of help to you.

Twenty-Five Sure-Fire Ways to Get Results

If you've read any of my other books, such as *The 25 Habits of Highly Successful Salespeople*, you know I don't like to mess around. I give you the information straight up—nothing fancy, nothing complicated. For this book I picked the format that has trained hundreds of thousands, if not millions, of sales professionals for nearly a half century. I selected the top twenty-five ways to relate to your team members, provide support when needed, improve performance, and get results. If you understand and pay attention to their needs, they will respond favorably, perform, grow, and want to stay in your organization.

With a little extra effort on your part, it is possible for you to create a galaxy of star performers who shine for years. I use the word *effort* because it took the universe some 13.8 billion years to evolve into what it is today. It's worth a few extra hours of your time to ignite a few stars in *your* universe, don't you think?

Do Any of These Folks Sound Familiar?

I begin the chapter by stating that today's sales professionals are a "puzzle." Review the puzzle pieces below and see if any of them sound familiar to you.

1. Melissa seemed to be really smart—but why does she seem to be unable to follow my simple instructions?

2. I keep telling Aaron he's doing a great job and he should keep doing exactly what he's doing, but he still insists on asking me for more feedback. It's driving me nuts.

3. In the past I was able to toss a how-to sales book to a new rep and she was off and running. Now every single sales rep keeps pressuring me about what training programs they should take.

4. My team is so energetic, except when it comes to weekly team meetings—it looks like they'd rather eat sand than sit there.

5. Jennifer is killing it with her sales numbers, but she never seems to be around. She comes in late because she has a yoga class, joins other teams in their brainstorming sessions, and leaves work early for some eco group meeting. My other reports think she's receiving preferential treatment—but she does get all her paperwork completed at night at home and never misses a target or deadline.

6. Devon is always going from desk to desk asking his teammates questions. Sometimes he needs their help, but other times he asks them what they're working on and offers suggestions. I'm not sure, but I suspect he's considered a nuisance and distracting.

In the above scenarios, here are the glaring issues:

1. Melissa *is* smart. Today's salespeople need instructions laid out and explained step by step. She expects her manager to walk her through it and provide frequent reassurances along the way.

2. Aaron may be doing a fantastic job, but he craves regular and consistent feedback. His confidence will falter if he doesn't receive specific details from his manager. He wants to be certain he's on track, and he's always seeking methods of improvement. He wants his manager to provide granular suggestions on what he's doing right, what he's doing wrong, and what he could be doing better— even when he doesn't specifically ask.

3. Employees born after 1980 thrive on training. They want to get their tasks 100% right and are excited to learn new shortcuts and tricks to get things done better and faster.

4. Managers who spend a half hour to an hour as talking heads during a team meeting will cause everyone to whack their snooze buttons. Salespeople in their twenties and thirties need to be engaged: meetings must be fun, interactive, and collaborative.

5. If the company's policies allow it, Jennifer—and the entire team—needs an approved and fair flex schedule that works for their job responsibilities. Salespeople today feel strongly about work/life balance. Everyone needs to understand and respect the parameters—for example, what hours are absolutely essential for Jennifer to be in the office and at her desk?

6. Devon is searching for more opportunities to work with his team, and there is nothing wrong with this in principle. One of his more experienced teammates might be good as a coach or mentor—something that could be formalized. Assuming that all of his regular work is done and acceptable and he's making all his numbers, Devon is ideally suited for a "stretch goal" on an approved team project with his peers.

These issues and many more are addressed and resolved in this book. Along the way, I provide helpful hints and tips in boxes (sidebars), numbered lists, bulleted lists, and a summary of the "Five Things to Remember" at the end of each chapter.

Relating to today's sales professionals isn't easy. But trust me when I say it's all worth the effort. Not only will you start to see results; your retention will increase, and your employees will be thankful that you finally "get them."

And, at last, your back bench will be filled with bright sales stars.

CHAPTER ONE

•
•
•

BREAKING THROUGH THEIR MINDSET

Recently, I was coaching and training a sales organization based in Portland, Oregon. As soon as I sat down with management and the sales leaders, they barraged me with their frustrations and helplessness in dealing with their young teams. These are some of the things they called out:

- They're really difficult to work with.
- They walk out when I'm talking to them or in meetings.
- They expect me to treat them as equals.

These managers were at their wits' ends. They couldn't believe these individuals had graduated from college and seemed good enough to be hired by their companies. There must have been something that made them come across as professional, smart, motivated, and capable. Where did all that go?

Let's take a step back. When you walked into the office on the first day of your first job back in the 18th century (okay, maybe not that far back), you were scared of saying or doing the wrong things. You went out of your way to show respect and be courteous to your boss. You desperately wanted to impress people and move up the ladder. You had every intention of staying in that company until you retired or dropped dead—whichever came first. You were probably thinking: "Wow! I have a job. This is great. People think I'm good enough and hired me. They're taking a chance on me, paying me a salary, and giving me benefits. I don't want to let my boss or anyone down. I want to show everyone what I can really do."

I have some news for you: the people you've hired as sales reps don't think being hired is any kind of honor or privilege like you did. If anything, it's the opposite. They think they can be hired by anyone at any time and leave for brighter horizons whenever they want. Whereas you were adapting to your company and boss when you started out, today's salespeople expect *you* to adjust to *them.*

You need to find ways to break through their mindset. And no, this doesn't mean preaching to them or berating them. Any preaching or condescending, hierarchical-sounding statements like "You need to pay your dues," "Know your place," "I'm your superior," "You have to toe the line," "Show respect," etc. will be treated with justifiable disdain.

Instead, if you have an employee who thinks he or she is an "equal" to you and not showing reasonable respect—i.e., not listening, eye-rolling when you speak, leaving meetings early, not following instructions—ask him or her the following simple question in a calm, casual voice: "How do you see my role here?"

The inevitable response will be a nervous chuckle followed by the honest question "Are you serious?"

"Yes," you reply in the same tone.

"Your role? Aren't you the boss? You make all the decisions around here."

"Okay, help me understand this. If I'm the boss and make all the decisions like you say, don't you think that what I say is important?"

"What do you mean?"

"Well, I asked you to format your sales forecast like everyone else. If you don't do it like that, I can't merge all the spreadsheets from the other reps to create the final forecast. If it doesn't get done right or on time, it reflects on the team's performance."

In the above instance, you've established a) that you are the boss and what that means; b) that the work needs to be done a certain way; c) *why* it's important to get it done that way; and d) *how* the employee's failure to follow explicit direction could hurt the team's overall performance and reputation.

The key in the above is letter "d"—*the team's performance and reputation.* Why? Because Millennials care about their peers and the team performance even more than they care about individual perceptions.

In their eyes, team failure is a personal failure. By recognizing this and pointing out that you understand this fact, you are getting into their mindset and earning their understanding and respect.

PERCEPTIONS OF LEADERSHIP: IT'S NOT THE OLD DAYS

It's a fact that years ago, businesses used to be a lot more hierarchical than they are today. The people at the top—the presidents, CEOs, CFOs, etc.—were barely seen, and were often on a separate corporate floor. If you did see an executive, it was a fearful moment in an elevator (assuming there wasn't a private one): What do you say that might make an impression? That individual had a certain presence about him or her and dressed the part: expensive three-piece suit and tie or designer dress and fancy jewelry with an anagrammed leather briefcase.

Businesses today are a lot more casual. You, your staff, and the head honcho may even be wearing jeans to work. You and the top boss probably intermingle and chitchat whenever there is an opportunity. As folks in dot.com businesses are well aware, some bosses don't even have their own offices and work right out on the floor with everyone else. If you are an outsider coming in for a visit, sometimes it's hard to tell who is in charge.

I'm not in any way saying this is right or wrong or that we should be longing for the "good old days." Today's casual environments certainly have many upsides: they are far less stuffy; they are a lot freer and employees have greater access to the leaders higher up the org chart; ideas and input from all employees are often welcome; and everyone seems *human*. These are generally good things that lead to a positive environment.

The downside is that there is an obvious psychological ramification to everyone seeming to be "equal." If everyone is out on the same floor, there isn't a "corner office" to strive for. If the boss is wearing jeans like everyone else, what's he doing with the extra money he makes if not spending it on clothes? Somehow the impression isn't the same.

Think about the culture of your workplace and how it impacts you and the team's perceptions. If you are on the floor with your direct reports, how do you behave to encourage perceptions of yourself as the leader in charge and not a control freak, micromanager, or tyrant?

One thing is for sure: there is nothing in the Millennial mindset suggesting that they care one iota about how things reflect upon you. They strongly disapprove of leaders who take credit for individual or team accomplishments and, on the opposite end, don't think for one second about how things might negatively impact you or your standing in the company.

When I was new to the workforce, there was a sense that you had your boss's back. You cared about your boss. You wanted your boss to succeed. His or her success meant your success. Today's salespeople believe you are impervious to harm because of your job title, and therefore you are on your own. They don't know or care about how you had to work your butt off for over twenty years to get to your position. They already believe they can do your job without having gone through the obstacles you faced.

Today, you don't need your team to refer to you as "Mr. Smithson," "Ms. Watson," or "Sir." (These actually sound ridiculous.) You don't even need them to call you "boss" (although it's kind of endearing if they do this on their own). You don't ever need or want to have a "superior" attitude when communicating with your team.

In general, you always want to include yourself as part of the team and say *we* instead of *you* or *I/me*. Your reps don't care about you, so if you use *I* they will presume you only think about yourself and not the team. Or, you are using yourself as an example to show you are better or smarter than they are. The collective *we* rings far truer.

Still, even though you want to exercise caution with pronoun usage, it can be extremely problematic for an employee to see you as an equal in other ways. There are many reasons why, but they have nothing whatsoever to do with your showing off your power and ego. It's about commanding respect, which is needed for the following reasons:

- **Decision-making:** Your employee has already admitted that you are the decision-maker. Since this is the case, there are times when it is essential that you must have unquestioned authority to make the decisions without worrying about "feelings" and "everyone's opinion" over what you think is best for the organization.

■ **Your expertise and experience:** Yes, this counts for a lot. You never want to remind them of this or shove it in their faces (yes, they will roll their eyes), but your years demand respect. By all means, acknowledge any areas in which they excel and you don't—i.e., technology is an obvious example—but that doesn't mean they should act as if your expertise and experience is of equal to or less value than the things they know.

■ **Leading the entire team:** If one individual doesn't show respect to you in front of the whole team, then the others won't either. It is fair for you to privately hold an employee accountable for any such behavior.

■ **Assigning tasks and responsibilities:** Without someone delegating projects and responsibilities, a team falls into chaos. While team members can request certain roles, ultimately you are the person deciding who does what.

■ **Performance reviews:** At the end of the day, you control that employee's destiny in the company. Will she get a raise? Will she get promoted? You never throw this in their faces, but during regular 1:1 meetings, it is always a good idea to keep employees apprised of where they stand vs. their goals and where their rating would be if the performance review were to be done that day. This is a great reminder to the employee that you are her manager, that you are not equals, without bluntly stating this fact. Your main goal in doing a periodic performance temperature take is to mentor and guide the employee, as well as to give the employee a reality check, as she may think she's 100% on track when that may not be the case. The reminder to her that you are the person who "rates" her performance is a residual upside for you in the process.

It goes without saying that everyone on the planet is equal in terms of importance and deserving of inalienable human rights. No one person is "better" than another. But when it comes to managing a sales team, there should not be a perception from anyone on the team that he or she is "equal" to the manager—even in a non-hierarchical workplace. You, as manager, are looked upon to coach and mentor your team and provide team members with the tools and support they need. But when it comes to decision-making and leading the troops, you are in charge and the one pressing them to make the deals, make sales, and make revenue. Without that understanding, they'll never listen to you and everyone will flop. If they don't perceive your place on the org chart, you have a respect issue with them and have to confront them head-on to change their mindset. Everyone needs to follow the road that you've paved—in the form of goals, targets, and strategies—to drive your company where it needs to go. The folks who venture down a separate path can just keep walking.

I've found that a key reason managers don't know how to manage today's salespeople is that they can't relate to them and can't get into their mindset. They become afraid to manage them because they come across as so convinced that they can do their jobs (which they can't). Throughout this book I will give you tips on how to bridge that gap. The first thing you need to realize is that some Millennial salespeople don't want to be managed in the traditional sense—and they don't want to be managed by you. Now that you are well aware of this incontrovertible fact, you can go about your business as manager doing what you need to do at the helm.

5 Things to Remember

1. Salespeople today do not see their managers as the same authority figure that past generations did.

2. Many young salespeople today believe that they are qualified to do your job without having had any experience as a manager.

3. Some salespeople see themselves as your "equal"; in fact, their roles are vital to the company, but you still need to demonstrate leadership to change their mindsets and reinforce that you are in charge.

4. You likely have team members who don't care how their poor performance reflects upon you, which means you need to associate everything with *team* success and failure.

5. Salespeople who don't respect authority and won't adjust their mindsets are welcome to test their theories out at another company.

• •
•

CHAPTER TWO

GETTING THEM TO BUY IN

In an ideal world, should you really be "obligated" to cajole your team into "buying in" to the product or service you are selling? No, you shouldn't have to do this. Are you going to end up doing it? You bet you will.

Millennials can be really skeptical and don't have a sense of the past. They also have an odd lack of imagination about the future, as if it's already arrived and they are convinced that they already know everything about it. They aren't paying any attention to the way things were, where they are now, and where they could be in the future.

The phonograph was an unbelievable invention in 1877. When Thomas Edison invented it, he had no idea how long it was going to last or be appreciated. It survived the cassette era and the 8-track era, sputtered during CDs, and vanished in the wake of digital music. The phonograph went kaput, right? Wait, not so fast.

In 2005, turntables came back, with sales of about 138,000. That's a pretty interesting blip. Was it just an anomaly? Between 2006 and 2014, the sales ranged between 60,000 and 111,000. The original excitement aside, this seemed like a pretty niche market that was flat to downtrending at best. But what happened in 2015? Sales went through the roof to *1.4 million!* A year later, sales reached *1.8 million!* Now, suddenly, we have a turntable trend, and records—*vinyl albums*—are a viable business once again. One company, SEV Litovel, is seeing 400% increases in turntables and can't keep up with demand.

You are probably asking: *Why are you bringing this up? Should I start investing in 8-track players?*

No, of course not. I bring up the turntable sensation as an example of how knowing the past can help the future. Today's sales professionals only see a big black cloud hanging over the future. It's absolutely ridiculous. They only see the negatives in the marketplace, not the opportunities.

I believe the past can often be a beacon to the future. When I get on a crowded bus, I can predict what is going to happen: some people will get off at the next stop; some people will stay on the bus; more people will get on. Am I a soothsayer? No. It's common sense. Business is circular, and customers are always coming and going.

Whatever you do, no matter where the bus is headed, you and your team don't want to be left off the bus because someone else—i.e., a competitor—has stolen your seats.

Your team needs to recognize that there are important moments in history, and this could be your turn to take advantage of them. How do you accomplish this? *Everyone must buy in 110% to your product or service and its bright future.*

Let's say your team is selling a widget that's existed since 1972. It still makes money and supports two thousand people in a factory, a warehouse, a back office, a sales team, a marketing team, a board of directors, and several executives. Sure, sales are soft and times are tough. They have *always been tough.* Your sales team is about to go off on a road show to unveil and present a brand-new widget that's been in development for years. One problem: your sales team doesn't buy in to the new widget at all. The objections might go something like this:

- Widgets are old—who cares about a widget?
- Anyone who wants a widget already has one.
- The competitors are outselling us three to one on widgets— how can we beat that?
- A new widget? Really? There's no difference between the old one and the new one. A widget is still a widget, isn't it?

What they are saying is that they don't buy in to your product, they don't believe in it, and they don't have any confidence that they can sell it. They couldn't care less that widgets have sustained the business for years and that the new widget is sensational. It's all doom and gloom and black clouds.

Do you think this sales team is going to succeed on a road show with this widget? Not a chance. They are guaranteed to fail. They've created a self-fulfilling prophecy. If they don't believe in the product, there is no way they will be able to sell it. The buyers will smell their lack of faith from a mile away.

ANOTHER WAY TO GET BUY-IN: CHARITY

Millennials tend to need incentives to "buy in" to the products or services they are selling. Many of them tend to have special interests in giving back to society and community through charity, which opens the doors to all kinds of possibilities. Your company might possibly sponsor a charitable event for a cause that is uncontroversial and that you know your sales team will support. It could also be an event that involves buyers and customers, so they can see firsthand how your organization gives back.

Other ways to get them excited about your product through charitable efforts might include financial contributions, fundraising events (such as a walkathon), doling out a certain amount of product to that organization for free, or offering a company donation of 5% or 10% of every purchase to that charity.

When your team members see that you are vested in the cause, they might develop more passion for the product and therefore push to sell more. They also might get more excited about staying longer with a company that has a charitable mindset.

Salespeople not only need fire in the belly in order to sell; they need fire in the brain as well. Their brain cells need to be bubbling with excitement over the new product. They should be pumped to hit the road: "A new widget? Hell, yeah—pile them high and wide, I can sell a ton of these!"

So, how do you foster this kind of enthusiasm? As a team exercise, gather everyone together for thirty minutes. To start the dialogue, show them a metal paper clip. Open with this:

In 1817 the paper clip was invented. What a brilliant, perfect invention! It's still used in offices everywhere—in spite of staplers, binder clips, and digital documents. The paper clip is never going away.

Now. Suppose you had to market and sell this metal paper clip. Your commissions depended upon it. How would you do it? Everyone knows exactly what a paper clip is and what it does, right? You're thinking: "He's out of his mind. Paper clips are old. Who cares? No one will buy a paper clip."

Ask everyone to write down their ideas for reinventing, marketing, and selling the paper clip. Anything that comes into their heads is fine. Each idea should be written on a separate Post-It. Give them ten minutes to come up with as many ideas as possible.

When time is up, have everyone place their Post-Its on the walls. Every salesperson should have at least ten, if not up to fifty. When they are done, the walls of the entire room should be covered with Post-Its filled with inventions, marketing ideas, and sales pitches for the paper clip. Pick a volunteer from the room to read them all aloud. I guarantee some will be silly, some will be wildly creative, and a few will be brilliant.

The point is this: everything has a precedent for invention and can be reinvented. Every year there is a newer and better smartphone. The reps at Apple are never going to whine "Aw, man, do I have to sell another iPhone again?!"

If Apple can create, market, sell, and generate excitement for new phones every year, why can't there be a newer, better paper clip? Think about the versatility of the paper clip today and all the variations currently available in office stores:

- Paper clips used to just be metal and come in only two sizes. Why not offer them in *ten sizes,* for every need?
- They could be made of bendable plastic instead of metal; no longer could they be used as sharp weapons or tear your paper when you remove them.
- Paper clips can come in a variety of colors—blue, green, orange, red, and more—so you can separate different documents by paper-clip color.

- How about an amazing low-priced paper clip spinner with dividers to separate the colors?
- Why not customize paper clips in the color and shape of your customers' brand and logo—it's a whole new revenue stream!

Whoa, that's a lot of stuff for just a paper clip! Imagine what your team comes up with! After the session is done, ask them to go off on their own and think about *the future of your company's product or service.* They can project all kinds of crazy things, which is exactly what you want. The exercise creates excitement and buy-in for your product or service because the salespeople have imagined all this unlimited potential on their own. The future will look bright indeed!

5 Things to Remember

1. Although you shouldn't have to get buy-in from your team for your company's product or service, sometimes you have no choice except to find ways to gain their enthusiasm and support.
2. Millennials tend to care much more about the present than the past and the future.
3. Your team needs your support to help them see the future potential of your product or service.
4. Charity can be a terrific way to get buy-in from your team.
5. Your team must emphatically believe that any product or service—no matter how tired or old—can be reinvented, marketed, and sold with success.

•
•
•

CHAPTER THREE

CONVINCING THEM THEY DON'T NEED APPROVAL FOR EVERYTHING

Millennials love being part of big groups at work and thrive in team environments where everyone is working together and pitching in. If they had their druthers, every person in the company would attend every single meeting so no one would ever get left out of anything. In their eyes and ears, everyone's voice matters.

In theory, this is a nice idea. What a utopia! Everyone has an opportunity to contribute and all opinions get expressed, heard, implemented, and duly credited. The problem is this: not everyone needs to be at every meeting, nor should every employee even feel the need to be invited or to invite others. Meetings aren't a free-for-all for people to become involved in matters not pertaining to their roles, functions, and goals (unless it's part of a developmental stretch goal as described in Chapter Twenty-Five). When that happens, employees believe they have a right to weigh in on *everything*.

What are the results? Unfocused employees, things get left undone, and decisions never get made because people start to turn the workplace into a commune where everyone has a say and a vote—and it must be unanimous or someone's feelings will be hurt. I'm sorry to be blunt, but it's business: *not everyone is going to agree with every decision, and not every decision requires every vote (or even more than one vote)*.

Sometimes a variation of this happens. An assistant who started in his first job three weeks earlier is invited to a meeting at which he bravely throws out an idea. People praise the idea and cheer him for it, but no one takes it seriously enough to get it started. What this employee doesn't realize is that he didn't need to be there at all; he was only invited to get to know people, feel like part of the team, and learn. It's great that he tried to contribute, but he shouldn't have any expectation that his idea is going to garner support; chances are, his idea was a distraction and those who praised it were just being polite and supportive. But why chew up precious company time in the first place?

My point is that a good deal of this "niceness" ends up going way overboard. Generally, a small group of people can get things done. You only need four or five people at a meeting, tops—not forty-five. No one should expect to be on a meeting invite or offended when not included on it. In fact, people should be thankful: *Hallelujah, one less meeting to attend!*

Part of the reason for this is that employees today are unbelievably anxious to get input and approvals from their peers on pretty much everything they do. I've seen sales teams listen to and trust their own teammates over specific instructions from their bosses and end up in the wrong direction. Democracies are fine, but not when it comes to sales teams who always need to *make sales*. I believe that all this conferring, consulting, discussing, and deliberating with each other without leadership only makes them more confused and less confident. They end up in a constant state of seeking approval and then hardly accomplish anything at all.

COMEDIANS DON'T NEED PRE-APPROVAL

Comedians make a living seeing things in the ordinary that others don't. They often say and do outrageous and unpredictable things to pry laughter out of audiences. Yes, comedians need "approval" in the form of laughter while on stage—but do you think late, great comedians Lenny Bruce, George Carlin, Richard Pryor, Don Rickles, or Robin Williams ever asked for anyone's "approval" before pushing the envelope with their routines? Never. If they did, not one of them would have made a dime in standup comedy. Their mothers would probably have spanked them for using such foul language!

There's a story I heard told by comedian/actor/TV host Howie Mandel. He happened to be shopping in a mall. A kid recognized him by his unique-sounding voice. Apparently, Mandel's regular voice is similar to the one he uses to play animated characters in a couple of different cartoons.

> The kid wanted to shake his hand and get his autograph. As the exchange happened, the kid asked Mandel how he could get away with using the same voice for two separate characters on two totally different shows. Mandel's reply: "The genius is not in the voice, but in *selling* the same voice twice."
>
> Did Mandel need anyone's approval to test out his theory in advance in the cartoons? No. He had the confidence to just go out and do it as he thought best—just like any great salesperson.

I hear it over and over again from managers that their team members don't trust or believe them when they say something. Sometimes the employees will go back to their managers four or five times with the same exact questions—and, of course, receive the same exact answers. If they don't get the repeated reaffirmation, they go straight to their peers and ask them. After surveying several people, a young sales rep will return to his or her manager and say "I know I asked you this before . . . but I've been thinking about it . . . and talking with Jen, Brittany, and Steve, who all think we should hold off on offering the discount to our customers. . . ."

Wait a second. No offense to Jen, Brittany, and Steve, but who said that their opinions were needed? Nobody. What a waste of everyone's time. If this ever occurs, you need to nip it in the bud—but without saying anything negative about Jen, Brittany, and Steve. The next time you speak 1:1 with your direct report, firmly say: "In the future, when I assign tasks to you and we discuss them, that's just between the two of us. I don't need to formally tell you it's 'approved' for you to start working on it. *Just do it.* Consider it approved when it's assigned to you."

The employee on the other end of your desk is probably thinking: *Well, what gives you the right to approve this by yourself—without any input from anyone else? Don't you want opinions from others? Won't it make it better if you do? What if you're wrong?*

Think about this: What gives *anyone* the right to do *anything*? I've now written over seventy books. I never asked permission or approval from anyone to write a single one. I didn't care what anyone else thought. I just wrote the books!

THE ACCIDENTAL MANICURIST/BLOGGER

I admit it: I'm an old-school sales guy. I get manicures. I believe a sales professional should always have well-manicured nails; it's part of making a good impression and presentation. If a customer sees you holding your product with dirty nails, it makes the product look dirty by association.

I have been going to the same manicurist for years. She does a great job and I like her. One day I went into the nail salon and found out that my manicurist had been writing a blog—a successful, popular blog at that.

I was impressed. I'd thought I knew her, and yet I hadn't had a clue that she had this whole other outlet on the side. I couldn't help but ask "Where did this come from? What made you decide to write a blog?"

"I don't know," she answered. "*I just do it.*"

If my manicurist doesn't need anyone's permission or approval to write her blog, your team doesn't need any approval to sell!

Sometimes your employees have such a need for constant approval that they question things over and over again without even getting started. These employees drag you into this and then cloud you with sudden doubts. *What if I don't know anything? What if it fails and I didn't check in with Jen, Brittany, and Steve? Won't I look foolish that I didn't allow my direct report to check in with them?*

Stop right there. You've made decisions many times over the years. You've been right and you've been wrong. This comes with the territory. Why would you think Jen, Brittany, and Steve have the knowledge or ability to decide this better than you? They don't. You are much better at what you do than you realize, but you falter when you get sucked into the "approval" demands of your reports.

Some of this need for approval can be attributed to how the Millennial generation was raised. You don't have to be a psychologist or sociologist to know that mommy and daddy watched over this group so carefully for so many years—probably past college when they still lived at home—and spoon-fed things to them. It's no wonder that they need approval for everything and can hardly do anything for themselves without someone's blessing. Endless hours of work time go by as they do nothing while waiting for everyone's approval. They need constant assurance that mommy and daddy said your direction is correct and okay to do.

Empower your people. Give them the confidence to do their jobs independently. They don't need to attend every meeting, nor do they need to invite every person to a meeting. A key responsibility of any sales leader is to maximize her employees' time so that they are spending most of it selling without distractions of needing input and approval from others—or spending all day doing that for others.

In short: *Permission and approval granted!*

5 Things to Remember

1. Recognize that your team's need for approval is not a reflection on you or your ability.
2. Keep the invite list for meetings small and meeting length brief: unless you are brainstorming or soliciting ideas, you are not there to solicit permission or ask for approval.
3. Guard your team from spending too much time in meetings and getting approval from each other.
4. Accept the fact that not every team member will agree with every decision you make.
5. Be confident that you are qualified and capable and have good judgment, even if your staff constantly questions you.

•
•
◦

TRAINING, TRAINING, TRAINING!

I'm going to take a wild guess and say that when you started out in sales, you received all of five minutes of training. Your boss shook your hand, showed you your desk and chair, went through some product details with you, handed you a manual, threw out some sales targets, patted you on your back, and said "Go get 'em, champ!"

All right, maybe you weren't thrown completely into the deep end of the pool without a float. Maybe you received *some* training over the years—like how to do an Excel spreadsheet or polish a PowerPoint presentation when those tools were brand new.

At the beginning of your career, you probably thought that sales training was a total waste of time. You already had the power, the cockiness, and the edge, and you could sell anything. You considered yourself a "natural-born salesperson," and everyone told you so. If your manager had suggested that you go to a training session, you probably would have groaned and then left his or her office feeling insulted.

"Training? *I don't need no stinkin' training!*"

Over the years, companies have recognized the benefits of sales training, and maybe you took—or were *compelled to take*—some sessions. (Maybe I was even your trainer!) Not just to become familiar with the products and the "company pitch," but also to hone certain techniques like cold calling and closing.

Now you're a sales manager, and the fate of whether your team succeeds or not is in your hands. Should you offer training sessions? Absolutely. Should your team be in training sessions 50% of the time when they could be out selling? *Absolutely not.*

Fast forward to today. You have a team of fresh and eager young recruits. They go through all the company onboarding stuff with Human Resources, and you do your best to bring them up to speed. You instruct and guide them about your product or service, the pitch, and all the Do's and Don'ts. It's entirely possible that your company has a few required training sessions for new salespeople.

All set, right?

Nope. Not with *today's* salespeople. Whether they say it or not—and whether they need it or not—your team wants more training! It could be a month or two years, or even five, but mark my words: *Young salespeople crave training.*

Huh?

That's right. Training. They need it and want it—even when it might not seem at all necessary to you. It's not necessarily inexperience, and it's definitely not lack of talent, confidence, or aggressiveness.

The reasons are actually pretty straightforward:

1. They always want to *learn more.* To them, learning is part of the work experience.

2. They are *competitive.* They're ambitious and want to get ahead, but this is a friendly competition. Think of how this group was raised on competitive video games with their friends in all forms: TVs, computers, and phones. They don't even care who wins the competition. This generation of people grew up expecting that they would get a soccer or baseball trophy whether their team won or lost. No one was made to feel bad if they lost, so on the whole they didn't care as much about winning as we did—or suffer the losses as badly.

3. They like the *interaction.* Salespeople today may be competitive, but they also enjoy sharing and hearing ideas. Yes, it's a social event outside the normal workday, and friendships can develop or be broadened. Mainly, though, in a training session chances are good they'll hear many of the same challenges they've been facing from their peers. If one of the trainees hasn't found the solution, the trainer is right there to help everyone all at once.

As manager of this team, your role is to *listen* and really *hear* their needs. In one-on-one sessions and in team meetings, ask them specifically what training they want or need. Write them all down on a whiteboard. Collect these ideas and repeat them back to the employees who suggested them.

Why? This shows you *heard them* and took the suggestions seriously. It demonstrates an important concept: *active listening.* Your people will feel that you listen and care.

BRIDGING THE GAP: WHAT IS "ACTIVE LISTENING"?

Human resources professionals preach "active listening" all the time. It's helpful for those managers accused by their direct reports of "not listening" or "not hearing" what was said to them, but it can also be valuable in client meetings.

I won't give you all the HR jargon. Simply put: you may *think* you are listening, but in reality the person speaking doesn't believe it. Why? Because you're giving the impression that you're doing something else instead of being focused just on listening. It could be that you're multi-tasking—an encouraged habit of Boomers and Gen-Xers. If you aren't talking over the person, you might be drifting off while the person is speaking. Even if you aren't daydreaming—you could legitimately be thinking of your verbal response too soon, or some other work dilemma—it comes across as your failure to pay attention. You assume you heard what was said—but did you really?

Active listening forces you to pay attention to *exactly what is said.* All you need to do is repeat it back word for word as you heard it: "I think I heard you say '*x, y,* and *z.*' Is this correct?" Or you could say "Tell me if I have this right. When you said '*x, y,* and *z,*' did you mean *A, B, and C?*"

By your doing this, your employee knows that he or she has been heard and interpreted correctly and knows that you care enough to have paid full attention and gotten it right. Young salespeople need to know that they have been *heard,* so active listening can be a good tool to use during any meeting situation.

But it's not entirely in your court, either. I'll bet you have to justify the expense of training to your own boss and make room in your budget for it. You can't make this happen just because your team members asked for it. Your team needs to *own* some of this as well and can't just throw it out at you to make it occur without sufficient ammunition. In the larger scheme of things, you, your boss, and the company as a whole have to figure out financial priorities. Is this particular training worth more than upgrading computer hardware for the company, for example?

Ownership of extra training means that you and your team both have a stake in it and the company can tangibly feel the benefits. A pitfall here is that you shouldn't make ownership seem like an assignment itself. Your employees may think you are "turning the request against them" by giving them more work. They may think it's a delay tactic for you to avoid advocating for the training and the expense. Like I said earlier, Millennials aren't stupid.

So how do you make ownership a win? Make it a brainstorming session. At a team meeting, write up all the suggested training needs from everyone. Stand back and let your team see everyone's ideas and soak them in. Then prompt them to state the specific need for each one and its benefits.

Let them go at it and collaborate. Write everything they say on the whiteboard. Try not to interfere with the dialogue, unless you're asked a specific question. Your participation here is to listen and guide; no decisions are being made on the spot. Resist the urge to give your opinion, which might sway the group or spoon-feed them. You don't want it to seem that you are influencing them in any way, as that will come off as controlling and bureaucratic.

Once the whiteboard is full and they've exhausted their ideas on training, be sure to offer specific praise based on what you heard. Remember: this was work for them and, again, you want their work to matter.

At this stage, you're probably ready to take a poll. You want to survey the team to prioritize the training sessions offered. You can do this by quickly going around the room, asking each individual to pick one session and then adding a checkmark on the whiteboard as a vote.

If you think a "private" vote is safer, by all means have each person write down their selection on a piece of paper. Read off each answer and check off the votes on the whiteboard.

Since people on your team may be at different stages in their careers or are responsible for different tasks requiring different kinds of training, it's okay if they disagree.

Add up the results. You don't need to make any decisions then and there. Thank the group again, and be clear that there will be more evaluation and discussion in the next few days. Your mission is to type up the whiteboard information right away and circulate it to the team before the end of that day. This shows you have a sense of urgency and are responsive to their needs.

You are next going to balance the outcome of the brainstorm session with your thoughts, which will probably include budgetary concerns and department goals. Whatever you are thinking the outcome might or should be, there is *always* a way to make training work and be productive. Podcasts, videos, and audiobooks might be workable and inexpensive options. Or sometimes you might have an expert right in your company who would be thrilled to lead a training session.

Your follow-up with your team is to pick the top two or three sessions voted upon and assign them to team members most passionate about each. Create a one-page proposal template for these individuals and give them the same reasonable deadline for completion. The template should include:

- Training required.
- Individual, department, and company need.
- Forum for training: i.e., one on one, team with trainer, virtual via video, or podcast, etc.
- Known sources for training.
- Anticipated costs, if known. (They don't need to price around.)
- Timing of training.
- Impact on the business: needs to be concrete with backup data: i.e., "will save 15% of time on each sales call."
- *Negative* impact on the business: i.e., investment in time, costs, etc.

Why is it so important that team members fill this out for training they want or need? Again, it goes back to ownership. The employee will figure out how important this training session really is for him- or herself, the team, and the company just by filling it out. It's also a learning experience for them. And, by seeing what's been written, you can determine how committed each person is to the respective training.

Once you have all the forms back, you can objectively review them against the budget and individual, team, and company goals. You can do more research on your own as needed regarding the specific training companies recommended.

You will then be able to make your decision. How does this training session rate against other priorities? How does it factor into achieving targets? Can you justify the value and benefits of the session to your boss, if you have to get buy-in up the chain? Might any of these sessions also benefit another department in the company or serve as a competitive advantage in some fashion?

Your decision is made. If you need to get your boss's signoff, you can write a memo with your recommendation and include your team's reports. Be certain to call out any individual's work you think is outstanding, so your boss recognizes your standout performers.

Assuming it's a "go" for a training session, you'll need to properly communicate that to the team. In doing so, thank them again for their efforts in the meetings and with the write-ups. Tell them their research was invaluable and this result wouldn't be happening without it. Make it clear that you spent a lot of time and energy on it and consulted with your boss on it as well for input.

As for the training sessions that were declined: where possible, *present the reasons why*. It could be that the timing is just off and that training would make more sense down the road. Or it could be purely an expense/budget decision; it doesn't mean the company is "cheap," it just means the money isn't allotted for training at this time due to current priorities.

Whatever you do, never imply that it was a "top-down" decision (even if it might have been from your boss). Your team will probably tar and feather you for having them go through all that deliberation only to have you or your boss toss it all out in favor of nothing or something else entirely. Trust me: it will be viewed as a power trip or whim.

If all training is nixed altogether—because of budget, timing, goals, etc.—be forthcoming with the team and provide the business rationale. Lay it on the line, but make it heard that you and the company regard training as vital. It's a matter of priorities, and they need to understand that. Give them a specific timetable for when you might be able to revisit training—and be sure to do it! If you don't, the team will bear you some resentment for it. They might even use "lack of proper training" as the excuse for not making their goals. It's unacceptable, of course, but you don't need or want to ever hear that.

Lastly, with regard to the training session selected: depending on the employee's goals, level, bandwidth, and abilities, you might want to assign the task of hiring and setting up the training session to the employee who proposed and fleshed out the idea. This continues to demonstrate ownership and becomes even more of a learning experience and growth opportunity for your sales rep. Don't make it feel like a burden, though; there could be *recognition* involved regarding a successfully executed training session, and it could serve as a model to other team members to volunteer as well.

If your employee sets up the training session, be sure to periodically ask how it's going. It's less of a bed check than an opportunity to mentor and guide your employee and see if you can lend a hand in any fashion. It might be the case, for example, that you personally know the trainer he or she is approaching and can offer some tips to shape the session based on your experience.

Most importantly, *listen* and *do not correct* (unless not doing so could cause a disaster). If your rep is making progress, let him or her run with it. Your employee is allowed to make mistakes and has earned the right to learn from them. After all, you made plenty of mistakes on your way up the ladder—and look at where you are now. Right?

We'll find out more about how to handle the training sessions themselves and make them engaging in Chapter Thirteen ("Conducting Team Meetings") and Chapter Seventeen ("Recognizing That They Know Way More About Technology Than You").

5 Things to Remember

1. Today's sales professionals need, want, and crave training even when you may not see the immediate need for it.
2. Bringing everyone together to brainstorm can help you assess the need for training and, if a case has been made, how training should be prioritized.
3. Let employees own specific aspects of the process to demonstrate their real passion for the training session.
4. Demonstrate active listening at all times with your team members.
5. Make sure to acknowledge and thank team members for having contributed to the process of determining what kind of training is needed.

•
:
⠄

INSPIRING TEAM SPIRIT AND UNITY

As covered in Chapter Three, Millennials need a lot of TLC, support, encouragement, and repeated approval from you to take the first step and initiate pretty much anything. As a sales manager and leader, you've probably given the "GO!" sign ten times to make a pitch, but feel like you're watching paint dry waiting for some people to pick up the phone or schedule an appointment.

In addition to needing all those layers of validation, your employees may be giving you *agita* over wanting to do *everything as a team.* This is not necessarily a bad thing, provided that the methods are productive and lead to results. As I mentioned in Chapter Three, you don't want or need every team member in every meeting. It's a waste of time for most people, can serve as a distraction, and also leads to churn with team members going back and weighing in on everything.

Another downside of a team that becomes enamored with each other is that they might pay more attention to each other's needs and goals than those of the company. The last thing you want is a team of salespeople rowing together in a direction away from you.

On the other hand, if you can channel and rein it in, team spirit and unity can be powerful assets for your department and for your company. If your salespeople enjoy working with each other, share valuable ideas and approaches, and learn from each other, they will head out to the field with greater confidence and sell more.

The first thing you need to realize is that your team of Millennials isn't being lazy, goofing around, or trying to procrastinate when they start up a schmooze-fest with each other. "Team play" is simply how they are accustomed to interacting—and you want to give them some leeway to develop a strong sense of camaraderie. But you also need to maintain a semblance of order, or things will get out of hand and you will have no control whatsoever.

Here are five things that can help inspire team spirit and unity, but also keep everyone focused:

1. **Establish a Team Vision and Mission:** These must reinforce the company's vision and mission. They can cull words from the company's vision and mission, but need to be specific to your group and long-term goals. Constantly remind them of your team's vision and mission and memorialize them in a central place, such as on your company's intranet. Every once in a while, you may wish to have team members spend fifteen minutes discussing the team vision and mission as a group and how your efforts have been feeding into them. The main thing is to ensure that the vision and mission are crystal clear and have been internalized by your team. They should be able to repeat them verbatim with pride to new employees and trainees. Note that vision and mission are separate from *purpose*, as explored in Chapter Twenty.

2. **Create a Wall Board with the Target Number:** In a prominent place in your office, post the target monthly/quarterly/annual number and update it on a regular basis with where the team stands and how much they have to go. Some organizations will ring a bell or use some other attention-grabbing device to trumpet a big sale.

3. **Turn Every Discussion into How to Hit the Number:** If your team loves schmoozing and brainstorming, fine. Just make sure that everything leads back to hitting the target number (i.e., as on the wall board in number two) for a specific product/service or making the month/quarter/year (whichever is of greatest priority—but be consistent). You want the team to unite and rally around the critical numbers. If they are going off on tangents, ask the simple question: "That's a good point. But what does it have to do with making our numbers?" Your job is always to bring them back and help them focus.

   The same goes for when a team member grouses about a sales challenge: don't let it turn into an all-out gripe session about the product, the marketing department, the buyers, or whatever. Reel it in and challenge the team: "How can we help Amelia get through this challenge? How would you handle this objection?" I would bet others on the team have faced the same obstacle at some point and have ideas on how to break through it. Your team would be more than happy to help Amelia out. At a certain point, summarize what everyone has said and ask Amelia to repeat it back so you know she "gets it" and the team feels satisfaction that they have succeeded.

4. **Celebrate Wins:** Take the time in meetings to acknowledge and celebrate success stories—especially when one team member helped another accomplish a goal. It doesn't take much for people to feel appreciated. Try to find out what your people like (don't assume) and reward them as a team. It could be as simple as bagels in the morning or a pizza lunch. Make a clear announcement about what the celebration is about. Be certain that if you celebrate one person's accomplishments, you must do it each time it occurs or people will get upset that you are picking favorites.

5. **Organize and Lead Off-Site Meetings and Brainstorm Sessions:** This is a terrific way to get your team excited and motivated, as long as you have a firm agenda (again, focused on making the numbers), share it with everyone beforehand and at the beginning, and stick to it. If team members try to derail a weekly meeting, you can say something like "That's a great idea for discussion at the off-site, Kyle—let's hold it for that. In the meantime, think about how it fits in with our goals."

GET A NINTENDO VIDEO GAME CONSOLE

We all know Millennials loved video games growing up. Many of them continue to play them as adults and regularly compete with each other during off-hours.

It should go without saying that you don't want your team playing video games at their desks on their computers, phones, or any other devices instead of working. You also don't want them spending the whole day in the break room (or whatever your office has) playing games all day.

However, if you make an organized contest out of it and have a specific day and time when they can play and compete, that can be a huge morale-booster.

If your company policy allows it, try investing in a Nintendo video console placed in a central location. Load up on all the Super Mario Bros games (or whatever, as long as it's not too violent, inappropriate, or loud) you can find, and set up a schedule for a Friday afternoon for the big team showdown. Dig up goofy prizes for the top three winners, and celebrate their victory.

If you're really brave, try to join in on the competition. Your Millennials will probably kick your butt in any video game, which is fine. They will see that you are human and have a thick skin, and they may even accept you as one of them.

Still, if you prefer to give yourself a fighting chance, go old-school and get a ping-pong table. Another upside of this is that it's physical (sort of) and can help people let off a little steam.

You may find yourself in something of a bind if you have team members who don't get along or jell and *don't* want to pal around with each other. Sometimes personalities just don't jibe, and what started out as a friendly competition between them becomes something detrimental to meeting team goals. There is nothing worse for a sales manager than having to play referee between two team members or adversarial factions. Disagreements are expected and sometimes even welcome, but an all-out feud can mushroom and spread quickly throughout your team and undo all your unifying efforts.

There are a few ways to handle this. One way is to sit them both down in a room and listen to them as they hash out their cases against each other. Your role is to stay quiet and listen until they are done, unless they start bickering and shouting—in which case you need to simmer them down and start all over again. When they're done venting (with equal time for both), ask them several questions to help them see each other's point of view. Enable them to recognize that they share more commonalities than differences.

Another method is to hold them *both* accountable. You don't have time to be a baby-sitter. You don't want to choose sides unless it's pretty clear-cut who is at fault and you have some corroborating evidence. A determining factor to see who has gone off course is to just boil things down to one question: *Which of the two parties is focused on the vision, the mission, the goals, and the numbers—and which one isn't?* The latter individual needs to be held accountable for going off-track and to be reminded of what is important.

There is also the possibility that you have a team consisting of a wide range of people between the ages of 21 and 70 (or more), and a dispute has arisen from the generation gap. You have a mix of Millennials, Gen-Xers, and Baby Boomers. That's usually a good thing: you want a deep, wide, and diverse bench of people who have the potential to turn into stars.

Unfortunately, the folks might not all get each other or see eye-to-eye. The Millennial might complain that a more experienced colleague is self-absorbed in his own sales goals vs. the team's and doesn't care about how his cocky behaviors are impacting everyone's reputation. By contrast, a Gen-Xer or Boomer might think that the Millennial is "getting away with being lazy" and is unwilling to learn from people with much greater experience.

These issues usually become visible and pronounced when the team is faltering and off-track. It's your job to unify your people and make sure you have clearly communicated *what* you are selling, *why* you are selling it, *what* are its benefits, and *whom* you are targeting. Remind them of the Vision, Mission, and targets/goals, and explain to all parties that these are shared and everyone is in it together as a team, including you. The thing *not* to do is draw attention to any age or generation gap within the team, as that can get dicey. You want to have an even keel and not play favorites, unless someone is off course or misbehaving.

However, here's what you *can* do: create a chart that breaks down into a half dozen or more sales attributes that are critical toward achieving your team's targets. Place one team member within each category. Make certain every team member has an identified strength (even if it can be debated) and leave your name off the chart. (This isn't about you.)

When you share it with the team at a scheduled meeting, state that you aren't implying that team members don't have more than one strength and wouldn't fit into more than one category. You have simply chosen a representative for each area and used your best judgment.

Now, give each rep five minutes to describe why he or she was identified with that attribute, and provide an example of it being used successfully.

This simple exercise is a strong way to highlight individuals' strengths and enable your employees to see and understand what everyone brings to the table. If, for example, you have a Boomer whose attribute is cold calling, she might tell a story about a successful cold call. If you have a Millennial whose attribute is providing product demos, she can demonstrate her style in front of the group.

This becomes a teachable moment for the people who aren't getting along, as well as for the entire staff. A team finds spirit when all members have a chance to see that everyone contributes something unique to the shared effort. They also feel a sense of pride in knowing that you recognize and appreciate everyone's strengths (without bringing up their weaknesses).

Thereafter, a Millennial team member weak on cold calling might independently do a check in with the Boomer cold-calling expert. Likewise, the Boomer who has trouble with the demos might ask for a pointer or two from the facile Millennial.

You may never have a 100% harmonious team. That's okay. Salespeople are aggressive and opinionated, and you want people who are passionate about what they do and aggressive about how they go about doing it. Workplaces are also like families, and we know most families don't get along with each other all the time.

If your salespeople learn to appreciate what everyone brings to the table, they will gain respect for one another, and then your unification efforts will start to take hold as you work together to meet your goals.

5 Things to Remember

1. Millennials crave team spirit and unity in order to succeed.
2. Periodically scheduled and organized off-sites and brainstorming sessions can help feed employees' need for team interaction and collaboration without derailing regular meetings.
3. Contests and scales scoreboards can be great ways to generate friendly competition in the office and unify your team.

4. If two employees are in a dispute, identify which individual is not focused on the vision, mission, and goals and hold that person accountable.

5. To help people of different generations get along, create a chart highlighting each team member's strengths. Have each person present his or her respective strengths with a real-life sales example.

.
.
.

CHAPTER SIX

ASSIGNING SALES MENTORS

Everyone can benefit from a mentor when joining the workforce or a new company. If you were lucky when you started out, you had a fantastic mentor who showed you all the ropes and boiled everything down to exactly what you needed to know. That person also spoke plainly to you and gave things to you straight, including areas where you needed to focus and improve.

I have a hunch that when you began your career, your first boss was your primary mentor. It may not have been a formal thing, but you looked up to him or her and learned from that person just by watching, listening, paying attention, and asking questions.

Some corporations have formal mentoring programs in which they set people up on "blind dates"—a senior-level person with a younger employee or a rising star—to try to match people up and iron out the latter's problem spots.

Some of these programs work, some don't. The biggest issue is always follow-through. Does the mentor set up regular conversations and meetings, or just blow them off? Or, does the mentee just go through the motions and not share the "real issues" with her mentor?

Mentorship is especially important for Millennials. Most of them crave the attention and need constant validation. The majority will appreciate that you took the time to think about them and offer the opportunity to have a mentor. It makes them feel special and important, and they'll feel good right away knowing that they have yet another sounding board.

The benefit to you as a manager is that assigning a mentor for an employee might free up your schedule a bit for other things. You may not have the time to provide all of your employee's much-needed re-assurance or, after a while, you sound to her like the voices of the parents and other adults in the Charlie Brown cartoons (*"wah-wah-wah"*). In other words, they're tuning you out.

Another voice and listening ear for your direct report can be of great help to you in getting the results you need. There may also be things lingering in the employee's mind about you, or there could be things she's just uncomfortable sharing with you. Getting those items aired out and resolved are vital for the employee's mental health and success, not just for your business relationship with her.

Sometimes people hate the word "mentee," as if there is a stigma attached to it. I don't get it at all. But if your employee needs and wants a mentor and you can accommodate it, call it whatever you want. For example, the word "buddy" might serve just as well.

You may or may not have influence regarding who becomes your employee's mentor. If you do, obviously you will want to work with your HR department to make sure it's a good fit and that the individual is positive, motivating, and can relate to the mentee's issues. You will want to try to have your employee matched up with a seasoned salesperson, or at least someone who has sales in her background and understands specific sales challenges.

If you have a good relationship with your HR director or associate, you might be able to start off by having a chat with your employee's mentor right at the onset. Although you want the employee/mentee to drive the program and her interaction with her mentor, you also want the mentor to at least be aware of your perspective. You don't want to say anything negative about the employee that can influence perceptions of their relationship; these are things for development to help the employee grow in his or her role and maybe move up the corporate ladder.

These are some examples of what you might want to bring up in your conversation with the mentor, presuming the mentee hasn't already shared them with you:

1. What obstacles are getting in the way of her sales efforts?
2. How can I (her manager/supervisor) be of greater help?

3. What opportunities for growth are missing?
4. Do you (the mentor) have tips/advice to help her focus even more?
5. Do you (the mentor) have tips/advice on handling sales challenges?
6. Have you had a chance to listen to her sales pitches?

Although you want to respect the relationship/privacy between mentor and mentee, it is still well within your right as manager/supervisor to do check-ins on a regular basis and see how it's going. Your employee may love hanging around with her mentor, but if they are heading off to Starbucks for two hours and shooting the breeze about the latest Netflix series and not dealing with issues of importance, it could end up being a nice waste of everyone's time.

Your check-ins should occur every now and then with your employee and become part of your regular 1:1 meetings. You aren't *prying*, you are demonstrating that you care and have interest in what she may be learning. All you need to do is ask "How is it going with Brenda?"

If your employee shares takeaways and progress with you, that's great. More often than not, though, it's like asking a fourth grader "What happened at school today?"

"Nothin'."

"Is everything okay?"

"Yeah, everything's fine."

The way to get around this is to ask her if she and her mentor are keeping track of goals and progress. You don't need to see these documents—especially if dealing with you is one of the problems on her list—but the employee should be held accountable for monitoring her own development. Once that conversation begins, she may decide to share certain ones with you, which can be helpful. You can ask questions; but try your best not to judge or provide input, as that can interfere with her relationship with her mentor.

On the flip side, you may also be able to check in periodically with your employee's mentor. Again, without getting into specifics, you can ask questions like:

- How are things going?
- Do you feel that the relationship is productive and making progress?
- Is there anything I can help you or her with?

I would bet the mentor will be a lot more forthcoming than your direct report about what is working and what is not working. I also doubt you'll hear Charlie Brown's parents saying "*wah-wah-wah*." This is the perfect opportunity to compare what the mentor and mentee are saying to you. They might be tracking 100%—or there might be a gap between them, in which case one person isn't being honest or forthcoming. Or maybe the whole setup is a waste of time. If that happens, speak with your contact in HR and see if it makes sense to end it. If she thinks it should draw to a close, try to have her bring it up with mentor and mentee. You don't want to come across as the bad guy who broke them up.

SHOULD ONE MILLENNIAL MENTOR ANOTHER?

No, not if you have any say at all in the matter. I think mentorships between peers, especial Millennials, inevitably become social forums and nothing will get done. They'll cheer each other on and provide all kinds of encouragement, but your employee will have gained absolutely nothing of practical use.

This is especially true in sales. Millennial team members may think they deserve a senior sales position and possibly even *your job* right out of college. When they start, they may not "get" the more experienced, senior salespeople. All they see is someone who is struggling to figure out how to connect his computer, can't properly fill in Excel spreadsheets, and hasn't a clue how to operate the company database. To a Millennial, the Boomer senior salesperson might even seem like an overpaid buffoon.

However, if that senior salesperson can take the Millennial under his wing as a mentee, the latter might learn what sales is all about. He might learn how to schmooze a challenging customer, close a difficult deal, negotiate seemingly impossible terms, or simply know how to shove aside a negative buyer decline and move right on to the next pitch.

Who knows? The relationship could even turn symbiotic and the senior salesperson will learn from the Millennial how to correctly fill out his Excel spreadsheets.

Still, as food for thought, if your employee is improving, progressing, growing, and selling more stuff since starting the mentorship, why interfere? Sorry about the cliché, but don't look a gift horse in the mouth. If it's working and the employee seems happy and is meeting or even beating her numbers, let it continue. *Something* is working. The last thing you want to do is deflate the employee and make her feel as if she's wasting her time. Perhaps the mentor is a better listener than you are or has better "validation words" than you do. Or, again, it could be things you've already said to her many times, but are now striking a chord because the words are coming from a fresh voice. If you are able to find out those magical words from the mentor, use them as reinforcement with your employee. I guarantee she will appreciate that you are learning something as well.

It's perfectly okay if at some point your employee wants to end the relationship with her mentor. That can go stale, and you don't want to keep it going just for the sake of it. It might have run its course. Or it could be that the assigned mentor was strong in some areas beneficial to the employee, but lacking in others. It's at that point that you or HR could consider assigning another mentor for the employee. It may sound overboard, but if the employee has talent and is strongly motivated, this is a small "give" to someone who has the potential of becoming a star.

5 Things to Remember

1. Encourage your Millennial employee to enter a relationship with a mentor.

2. If you have any say in the matter, set up your Millennial with a seasoned salesperson.

3. Allow the employee the space to develop her own goals with her mentor.

4. Try to serve as a "consultant" to the mentor/mentee relationship, but don't overstep your bounds and interfere—especially when it comes to information the two have shared in confidence.

5. Pay attention to "learnings" from the mentor or mentee that could help you manage the latter better.

CHAPTER SEVEN

•
•
•

CONVEYING THEIR TARGETS

Companies can vary in terms of when they start to create the revenue budget for the following year, when it gets finalized, when it receives the official signoff, and when sales quotas are assigned. No matter when the last stage occurs—August–December for the upcoming year, or Q1 of the current year—there is always a push/pull that goes on in terms of what the team can easily accomplish vs. what might be considered a "stretch." The people at the top will never set a bar too low, but they have been known to make it pretty high—maybe even way up in the clouds and seemingly unreachable. The main idea, of course, is that every target should be fair and aggressive, pushing salespeople until they might bend a bit—but not break.

The *who, what, how,* and *why* of the sales targets are sometimes within the sales leader's control and sometimes not. Hopefully, when you are in this position, you have at least some say in the matter and can determine how the quotas get divvied up and assigned. If you happen to be the person who establishes the targets, the thing you should never do is set them to please your Millennial team members or get their approval. You shouldn't set light goals for certain people because you are worried about how they might react. You need to be fair—and this is your call, not theirs.

At the end of the day, you are also the one who is *communicating* these targets—the company's, your team's, and at the individual contributor level—so it's critical that you handle it right.

When it comes to today's young sales force, your mission in communicating the targets is less about getting them to buy in to it and feel confident than it is about getting them to pay attention to it at all.

The company number, the team number, and the individual number may seem vague and unreal to a Millennial. Some of them might feel like they deserve extra commissions and bonuses just for showing up to work every day.

The thinking is that everyone should get rewarded, right? If the company makes its goal and the team makes its number, then shouldn't everyone share in the reward?

Nope. Individuals need to understand that a) the company and team goals are important, BUT: b) your reward is solely based on your results. This seems obvious to old-school salespeople, but not so much to Millennials.

The first order of business is sharing information as early as you can with the team. Help them feel involved and part of the process, even if the numbers are handed down from the executive team. You want to give them as much of a "heads-up" about what's coming, with the caveat that it may not be final and is subject to change until official signoffs.

WHAT IF THE NUMBERS ARE HANDED DOWN FROM MOUNT OLYMPUS?

There are many corporate sales organizations—perhaps yours is one of them—in which the goals/targets/quotas (however they are phrased in your business) are sent to the entire sales force all at once via e-mail with minimal, if any, explanation. The marching orders have been handed down from Mount Olympus, and the mortals (including you) must live with them for the entire year. They are what they are— end of discussion.

At first, your longtime reps bitch and moan to their computers (or buddies, if nearby): *"Thirty percent increase?! They're f–n crazy!"* Then they roll up their sleeves and figure out how they are going to do it. Forty years ago, they swilled down some whiskey before pounding the pavement.

The Millennials? Nuh-uh. When they receive that blanketed command from Zeus, Hera, and Hades, they get completely lost on Neptune.

Whether you participated in the company, team, or individual quotas, it is still your responsibility as manager to review them with the entire unified team. The senior salespeople won't need such babying, but include them anyway in the discussion, as they can help lure some of the younger deer away from the headlights and provide reassurance just by saying "*No problemo.* Been there, done that. We've got this."

Don't stop there! Afterward, speak with your people in person 1:1 or on the phone, if they happen to work at another location. Let them vent their concerns, answer their questions, and coach them. Do regular check-ins.

If you fail to do this, you might lose employees to other companies simply because the headlights were too bright for those deer and you didn't do enough to support them. The slightest amount of encouragement will go a long way toward showing them that the company (and you) cares about their success and future.

The next stage is explaining the *how* and *why* of the numbers. You need to prepare for this as best as you can in advance so your team doesn't poke holes in your explanations (or in the math). Make sure the meeting is only about the targets and nothing else and you have enough time to go through everything with enough detail. You don't want the meeting to end with anyone being confused because you didn't finish or there wasn't enough time for questions.

The *how* is not about "how they will achieve the numbers," but how the targets were originated; in other words, the logic behind them. You want to back your statements with hard data. For example, if a certain account has been growing at a rate of 3% each of the last three years, you might explain that overachieving with a 4% increase is expected of a world-class sales team like yours. Or the advertising/marketing budget for the product has gone up 10% from the year before, which means the sales targets have been raised to match the investment. Increased advertising/marketing spending means that more sales should be expected, right?

The *why* may seem simpler, because it would be easy to say "Tough noogies, the numbers are the numbers because that's what the CEO wants." Well, that never gets support from the sales trenches. Similarly, you don't want to lay the corporate-speak (i.e., BS) on too thick or you will come off as a phony—especially to a team consisting primarily of Millennials, who will see right through you.

Here's what you do. When presenting and sharing the targets, go in with 110% confidence and 120% transparency. You need to convincingly get across that you believe in the targets yourself (even if you have doubts or were overruled on something), that they are doable, and that you are all in it together—even though there are important individual goals that must be made. You are right there beside them every step of the way.

Then boil the *why* down to something easily digestible: "Here's how the decision went down. Last year we beat our numbers by 5%. A few people on the executive team think the bar was too low last year and we just did a lay-up. So this year we set the targets 6% above where we expect to land. This way, we can really show them what we can do and that last year wasn't a fluke."

When the *why* has been communicated, go step by step through your prospecting process to work out the math together with them. Based on the data, how many prospects will they need to have and convert in order to make the numbers? (We'll go through this in greater detail in Chapter Eight.)

Lastly, make sure you have time for pressing questions. Some people may be upset with the numbers and start venting: "How can I possibly make that? My account just closed ten stores—they're cutting back on everything."

Acknowledge the issues they raise and take them seriously. Give them a chance to vent; they are, after all, hearing these numbers for the first time and are processing them. Try to anticipate these questions in advance and have honest, realistic answers at the ready. If you can't respond to an obvious question, you will have zero credibility and you and your team risk doing a belly flop in the shallow end of the pool then or by the end of the year.

That said, leave room for the chance that someone on your team makes a valid point—one that might mean you need to go back to the drawing board and/or re-discuss the sales goals with your superiors. Mistakes and oversights can and do happen. If a disparity is pointed out and you can't resolve it on the spot, the worst thing you can do is to push back or defend that position, as you will lose credibility. Instead, thank the individual for being so astute and say you'll work on it some more and get back to her. When you do return with revised targets, once again thank the team member who brought it up, and highlight what changed and why. By doing this in front of the whole group, you will come across as trustworthy and supportive of the team, and there is a greater chance that they will make a strong effort to beat the targets.

Think you're done explaining the targets? Not on your life. Whereas old-school sales reps may have had their numbers emblazoned on their foreheads, today's salespeople need constant reminders. This isn't because they are forgetful, but rather to keep them first and foremost in their thoughts. In 1:1 meetings, therefore, restate all the numbers: both the *how* and the *why*. Ask them to repeat them back to you. You'd be amazed at how many reps misunderstood the targets, or were going with "old" numbers since they were updated and replaced.

Are you done yet? Still no. Go through the annual targets on a monthly or bimonthly basis with your team. Remind them of the *why*. This becomes especially important because priorities shift and things do happen over time to distract focus. There could be a shortfall one month or one quarter, and some reps might make the erroneous assumption that the annual target has been lowered when it hasn't. If a change does happen from when the numbers are first presented, go over them again and again to be certain the team knows which version is correct and the most up-to-date.

In some circumstances, Millennial sales reps may decide on their own that a reforecast during Q3 to reflect actual sales to date means that their annual targets have softened and been decreased. *Au contraire!* The revenue budgets and targets were locked and loaded months earlier, which means the reps' commissions and bonuses remain forever tied to them. The revenue forecast, by contrast, needs to be as accurate as possible to help the Finance team and the Executive team figure out what needs to be done (i.e., a shortfall might mean a budget cut), but the original targets never shift.

Think of it this way: If a marathon runner gets a cramp on mile 24 of a 26-mile race, the length of the course doesn't suddenly shrink to 25 miles—does it?

5 **Things to Remember**

1. Set aggressive sales targets for your team that are doable but won't "break them."
2. Present the quotas as early as you possibly can and with believable conviction.
3. If management handed down the quotas, take the time to explain them to the team and give everyone the opportunity to process them and ask questions.
4. Always back up *how* the targets were created with real data.
5. Constantly remind the team of the quotas and why they are important.

·
·
·

CHAPTER EIGHT

GUIDING THEM ON PROSPECTING

Sales success is determined by one thing: the ability to effectively mine your prospects. If your team isn't securing enough appointments, you'll never have a chance of reaching your targets. It all comes down to a formula I've proposed in the past:

$$A = P = S \text{ Formula}$$
Appointments give you *Prospects,* which give you *Sales*

Your Law of Ratios dictates that you need enough appointments right from the outset to lead to prospects. From that pool, you develop your sales. It's simple math. Suppose you contact 500 potential customers (via any method, such as e-mail, cold calling, etc.) and average a 10% conversion rate to meetings. That means you have 50 appointments to work with. If you average closing 50% of all meetings, you are looking at 25 deals out of that initial pool of 500.

Your goal is to sit down with your team and make certain they have enough leads to generate the needed amount of sales. Are the aforementioned 25 deals enough to make your targets? If not, your starting number of 500 potential customers needs to be increased to 750, 1,000, 1,500, or more.

An additional point of reference is targeting the source of the *highest revenue-generating customers* and focus on them. For example, if you know that customers in a certain territory buy more (or have a higher percentage of conversion), you need to focus more energy on getting appointments in those areas—which may mean you can reduce pressure to get appointments in the less-productive areas.

But what about the *method* of sales outreach? Is e-mail the be-all and end-all for getting appointments?

Barbara, a long-time VP of Sales, was struggling to figure out what was happening with her team. According to the data and metrics, the team's number of leads was up 15% above the prior year per rep—and 10% higher than the year before that. And yet the conversion rate was down significantly across the board—some 25%—which meant that their overall sales and revenue were down year over year.

This didn't make any sense to her. What was going on? How could more leads mean *fewer sales*?

Barbara sat down with her team: Max, Alexa, Jessica, Ethan, Amanda, and Christopher. She asked them to anonymously write down on a sheet of paper how they outreached their leads for the first point of contact. She said "Don't think about it too much. It's not a trick question. Just write down how you first contact a lead in most cases, and then pass your paper forward."

Half of them didn't hesitate to write down an answer and push their papers forward. The others evidently continued to regard it as a trick question and struggled. Alexa and Ethan gnawed on their pens until they finally wrote something down and handed in their sheets. Max—now the lone holdout—kept crossing out his answer and ended up crumpling it up and starting over with a fresh piece of paper, which caused the others to laugh at his expense.

"Come on, Max," Barbara implored him. "Just write down an answer."

He turned red, shrugged, and scribbled something down, shoving the paper across the table.

Barbara mixed up the papers, in case anyone in the room might think he or she was going to be identified and singled out. Of course, she could have recognized someone's handwriting—but the truth of the matter was, she didn't care who wrote what.

She read each answer aloud, one after the other: "*E-mail. E-mail. E-mail. E-mail. E-mail. E-mail.* That's six out of six."

Barbara was stymied. She had no idea that *all* their leads were being contacted primarily by e-mail. She panicked: *How on earth are we going to convert those into sales if all we are doing is sending generic e-mails?* Then she realized that their e-mail lists had been severely taxed and they were pounding the same people over and over again with the same e-mails. No wonder their conversion was declining at such a rapid rate.

Based on the statistics, Barbara should not have been so surprised. According to a recent study by ClickZ, 73% of Millennials prefer e-mail outreach as the primary method of contact. This is not necessarily a bad thing on the surface: e-mail is a valuable tool for sending out a message immediately, for tracking communication, and for weeding people out who have left their companies (which come back as undelivered). E-mail is also incredibly cheap and easy.

However, in driving sales, it should not be the only way to approach leads. Picture yourself as a buyer or purchasing agent for a company. How many times have you ever received an e-mail pitch and stopped everything you were doing to exclaim "Wow! Stop the presses! This is just the e-mail we were waiting for! We absolutely have to buy this right now!"

The reality? We all know this never happens. When it comes to first-time outreach, e-mail often fails for one or more of the following reasons:

1. People are bombarded by e-mail 24/7. There is just too much going into their inboxes, and yours is destined to get lost in the morass along with all the other pitches.
2. Many e-mails end up being blocked as spam or relegated to the junk folder on the other end with the sex ads, weight-loss products, and miracle supplements.
3. If the recipients don't know you or your company, there is a strong likelihood that they will identify it as a "pitch" and delete or ignore your e-mail right away.
4. If the leads regard the subject line as poor, the e-mail will be ignored or deleted right away.
5. If the recipients do get past the subject line, they still might hate the generic body-text copy and ignore or delete the e-mail at that point.
6. If the recipients are in a really bad mood from your subject line, your copy, or both, you might be blocked from sending future e-mails.

7. Whether or not your e-mail is blocked, sent into the junk folder, or deleted right away, the recipients still get an impression that your company is far afield from their company's needs.

8. Your competitors are doing the same thing as you—bombarding them with e-mails! You are getting lopped into the same grouping.

Above are the practical things that can go wrong with e-mail as the first form of outreach. There are also several critical things missing from e-mail as the first point of contact:

1. **The personal touch:** Your reps never get a chance to know the buyers and vice-versa.

2. **Questions:** Your reps don't have the chance to ask questions and find out the buyers' needs.

3. **The pitch:** You can't switch gears in an e-mail. You have one shot to get a buyer's attention and convey everything you can do for her company, and that's it.

So, knowing all this from all her years of experience, what should Barbara do with her team? Simple: she needs to train the team on going old-school. Mainly, what is wrong with a telephone? Every time one of her team members picks up the phone, she gets closer to a "yes."

I've written many books on cold calling (or the icky word "telemarketing"), and I believe it's still the best way to get a foot in the door. Think about it. For today's generation, the phone is the single most important thing in their lives. They use it for texting, running apps, gaming, engaging in social media, chatting—everything *except for calling people and speaking to them in person.* Isn't that what a telephone was originally invented for? Imagine: you can teach them that the phone they carry around with them as if their lives depended on it can actually be used to speak to another person—*live!* How remarkable!

You may have a hard time convincing your team about the value of actually making a phone call on a phone—especially to someone he or she doesn't know. It can be intimidating, for sure, especially for Millennials who don't gab on the phone for hours with their friends the way we used to.

Well, guess what: speaking with other people is the job of selling—not just clicking send. Otherwise, robots could do it (and, shamefully, we are getting there already).

If Barbara's sales team were to pick up their phones and call leads, there is no doubt they would get a fair share of wrong numbers, out-of-office messages, and statements along the lines of "Bill left the company" or "Karen no longer handles that." Fine! That's an opportunity to get the correct numbers (the Internet is a treasure trove of answers!), leave a compelling voice-mail message, or find out directly from the person answering the phone who is the replacement and current buyer/purchasing agent/contact.

If, however, buyers do answer the phone or call back—which some will—this is an opportunity to roll up the sleeves and make some sales. The first thing is finding commonality with the person on the other end: *Do you know some of the same people?* The second is finding out some things about the buyer: *How long have you worked there? Is business good?* Small talk might work here ("Did you watch the Super Bowl? What a game!") to find out interests and turn up the charm. The third thing is asking questions: *What challenges are you guys facing with x, y, and z?*

Note: In the above questions, the rep hasn't even begun to pitch the product or service! It doesn't in any way sound like it's a sales call (aka cold call). She is *finding out information.* She is *demonstrating that she cares.* She is *listening to the buyer's needs.*

Then, guess what? If the buyer seems receptive, the rep can swoop in and introduce the product or service by tailoring it to everything she just heard. In other words, she can *solve the buyer's problem.*

The call doesn't at all need to be a hard-line pitch. The rep, who has a foot in the door, should then try to open it all the way by setting up an in-person meeting. Why? Because face-to-face is always better than phone—and phone is typically better than e-mail.

Of course, e-mail is a great *second* tool to use as follow-up. It's the ideal way to restate what the buyer said in the conversation (i.e., state the challenges) and reinforce how you responded to her (i.e., how you would solve the problem). This is the perfect communication method to firm up details of the in-person meeting, tailor/refine the marketing pitch (based on all the information gathered during the call), bring up any new information that helps the pitch, and send materials about your product and service as attachments.

Let's get back to Barbara, as she still might be struggling to persuade her team to press numbers on their phones and talk to people. It's time to do a trial run. She needs to evenly divvy up 140 leads (or whatever number, but make it a significant pool) among seven people. Why seven? Because she is going to take on twenty leads *herself*. This way, she can show she's in the trenches alongside the others and is one of the team.

THE END OF COLD CALLING?

In late November 2017, The Daily Sales website posted an article by Daniel Disney titled "Millennials Will End Cold Calling by 2025." Mr. Disney makes a compelling argument. Things certainly seem to be heading in that direction.

But that doesn't mean that you and your organization should throw in the towel! If you can train your team on how to make pitches by phone and in person, you will have a significant advantage over the competition. The Millennials may resist you on this, but if you show them its effectiveness vs. random e-mails and demonstrate that it's the right way to add to their community, they will fall in line.

Once the buyer relationship is in place, phone calling and face-to-face are still important, but e-mail can take care of the day-to-day for the most part. Your Millennial reps are free to e-mail, text, or even link with their buyers on social media (as long as they are smart about this and don't post stupid and/or off-putting things). There is no doubt that these are the areas where their skills far exceed yours, so let them have at it at that point.

She should make it a fun contest: Millennials love friendly competition, so why not make a game of it? Offer prizes (such as movie theater tickets, dinner vouchers, Starbucks cards, etc.) not just to the person who converted the most sales, but also to the one who has the most in-person meetings set up. (She should, of course, exclude herself from the contest and winnings.) She can set up a firm date with enough time (about a month—she shouldn't stretch it out too long) for everyone to get through his or her list. Each rep should fill out a simple sales-call sheet (or use the company's tracking system, if there is one):

1. Name, title, company, contact information for the buyer, date/time of call.
2. What information did you gather about the buyer—length of time at the company, personal info of value? (Married? Kids? Areas of interest?)
3. What challenges does the buyer have?
4. What solutions did you present?
5. What was the buyer interested in/not interested in?
6. If there was an immediate decline, what was the objection? Was there a chance to overcome the objection?
7. Follow-ups: e-mail, in-person meeting, another phone call, send materials, etc.

When the deadline is up, Barbara should make it an event. She can offer some snacks that she knows the group will enjoy. She can set it up as a sharing/brainstorming session and even invite senior execs to attend.

Barbara will open the meeting by tallying up the results and awarding the prizes (excluding herself, of course). Then she would list the raw results on the whiteboard in columns:

1. No response: phone number doesn't work, employee left, etc.
2. Conversions: number of sales.
3. Declines: how many just said "no."
4. E-mail follow-ups.
5. In-person follow-ups.

These columns of data are fascinating points, of course, and Barbara should let everyone in the room soak them in. But then each rep would be given a turn to go through their learnings from each of the calls. Naturally, everyone would find out a lot about reactions to the products and services being offered: Were they liked? Disliked?

Along the way, the attendees will learn a lot about all the prospects who were contacted. Barbara will also discover a great deal about how her team members operate. For example:

- Which reps put the effort in?
- Which reps became enthusiastic about the effort—even if they might not have been at first?
- Which reps were easily discouraged?
- Which reps have the gift of gab on the phone?
- Which reps are good listeners?
- Which reps can close deals?

The exercise should not end there. Reps should continue to make calls to each prospect, even if it might be frustrating. Hang-ups and slammed doors on noses are par for the course in sales and everyone—including Millennials—needs to learn how to face declines and be both tenacious and resilient.

The long-term upside of initiating the sale by phone is that the rep is establishing a *relationship*. Each salesperson should contact the buyer periodically—even if there is no agenda—just to see how things are going. By getting to know the buyers personally, the reps can anticipate what they might like in the future—if not ask them outright—and know how to present and handle issues before they occur. In doing so, the buyers know the reps have their backs and trust them.

THE BEST MOVIE SALESMAN

Remember the late John Candy co-starring as Del Griffith, the lovable but somewhat annoying hanger-on to Steve Martin in the comedy film *Planes, Trains and Automobiles*? Del sold *shower curtain rings* for a living. Really! Go back and watch it for the billionth time. He actually made a living selling *shower curtain rings*.

Del has a certain amount of "regular guy" charm, but it's his in-person pitch that makes him a great salesman. (Most certainly *not* the product!) When we see him in action, he spouts clichés like "This is the deal of a lifetime!" with unbelievable passion and sincerity. He also thinks on his feet, being able to change the value proposition of his priceless shower curtain ring on the spot to anyone, depending on the person he is selling them to. The shower curtain ring becomes "Diane Sawyer's earring," "Czechoslovakian ivory," "a Walter Cronkite moon ring," an "autographed Darryl Strawberry earring," and valued objects that "were handcrafted by the great wizards of China back in the fourth century."

People plunk down all kinds of cash for his worthless shower curtain rings. But who could resist such cheerfulness?

Think about it, though. Would you want to limit Del by selling your product or service via e-mail? No way. Get him pounding the phones! Or, better yet, send him out by planes, trains, or automobiles to meet with buyers immediately!

On the other hand, if the relationship has been formed 100% by e-mail, the rep will know next to nothing about the buyer (and vice-versa). When a problem arises, the rep won't have a clue how to resolve it with the buyer, because she knows nothing about him or her.

Imagine using the personal touch vs. the competitor's approach— which is probably all via e-mail: Don't you think a buyer would rather have a real person she knows fielding a challenge than a disembodied e-mail recipient?

Your team may not believe you, but prospecting and following up on leads are the *fun* parts of the job. This is all about the hunt! For many Millennials who love to text and hide behind emojis, they can be led to the water by letting them know that hearing a genuine voice and seeing a real face not only brings them more sales—it adds substantially to their valued community of contacts.

5 Things to Remember

1. *Appointments* give you *Prospects* which give you *Sales*.
2. E-mail should not be the sole method of customer outreach for appointments.

3. Train your team on cold calling—odds are they have no idea how to do it.
4. Make a contest out of cold calling to show them its merits.
5. Encourage the reps to use e-mail, texting, and social media as follow-ups—but not to replace speaking by phone as a communication method.

.
.
.

BROADENING THEIR SALES COMMUNITY

I've found that, even once you've guided a team on using the phone for outreach as explained in Chapter Eight, there are still challenges for sales teams today in terms of widening their contacts to broaden their sales community. While Millennials are socially driven and love "community" (*social media* community, that is), it can often be difficult for them to "break in" and establish viable, lasting connections that aren't just digital.

There are lots of things you can do here, but ultimately the key is finding the right motivation and then tapping into it. One of the things I've noticed is that, since the Great Recession and the continuing digital-communication explosion, trade shows are starting to become a thing of the past. Companies have been scaling back participation in them due to cost vs. tangible ROI. I can't say I blame them: trade shows are costly—renting space, building booths, creating marketing materials, paying for employees' airfare, cabs, hotels, meals, drinks, etc.—and can be a big time drain with everyone out of the office for a week (and tied up in the prep beforehand and follow-ups thereafter).

I'm not going to try to convince you to rethink your company's position on trade shows, especially if you've already written them off as unnecessary burdens. If you have forgone the extravagant booth, that was probably a wise choice.

However, think of all the years that you attended trade shows and all the people with whom you met and bonded. Sure, it was largely social stuff and not necessarily tangible revenue generation, but those interactions built some of your longtime business relationships and friendships that you wouldn't trade for anything. Admit it: after a day's show closing, you loved going to the bars and pubs with these buddies and downing a scotch, vodka, beer, or whatever your beverage of choice was. You'd kick back and catch up with your buyers, customers, and partners.

The current generation is probably hearing things like "trade shows are a waste of time and money" and "no one goes to them anymore." But deep down, you have to believe they are curious about what goes on at them. They would love to be part of something bigger in your industry and hobnob with other industry professionals. It might even afford them a rare opportunity to meet with company executives. Perhaps they'll commiserate with other salespeople and learn a trick or two. Or, they'll see how competitors market and sell their wares vs. yours and bring back some good intel. Better yet, maybe they will develop new business on the fly that otherwise might not have occurred, or even pick up on a new business trend.

You're still probably thinking: "Oh, man, that Schiffman guy wants us to go back to the old days and spend tons of money for people to drink and smoke cigars." No, no, and no. (I'm not saying that this wouldn't be fun. . . .) Instead, I'm suggesting that there are numerous ways to involve your reps in trade shows for the experience, while still getting bang for your buck and keeping your team focused. Here's the strategy:

1. **Select minimal attendees.** Every year, choose one or two people to attend—tops. Rotate attendees each year. Those who don't get selected the first year, assure them they will attend the following year. (Trust me: there will be jealousies.)

2. **Watch the dollars.** These are reasonable things to look into:

   - *Day trips:* One day or one day/night might be all that is necessary.
   - *Monitor flight costs:* There are low fares all the time. Book far in advance to find deals.
   - *Hotel costs:* There are almost always reasonable options, albeit the best ones are usually not within walking distance of the convention centers. Some companies have employees (of the same gender, of course) share rooms. It might be uncomfortable for

some people—but it's a reasonable thing to suggest if you are on a tight budget.

- *Badge costs:* Sometimes the shows have "early-bird specials" for badges with lower fees. Or, if your budget is really tight, sometimes you can get away with employees sharing a badge and switching off entry. (If you get caught, don't tell them Stephan Schiffman recommended this!)
- *Meals, drinks, etc.:* Give your employees a daily budget. Most employees will adhere to parameters when they are specifically outlined in advance.

3. **Pre-planning.** Each attendee must do prep work for the trade show. It's not a free ride. (Well, it is . . . but it's not a *vacation* ride). The employee must create a list of goals and the names of people he or she intends to either outreach for an appointment or try to meet up with at the event. As supervisor, you need to challenge each employee to come up with at least three solid goals and show you a full meeting calendar of appointments beforehand (with buyers and movers and shakers). You could even take this a step further and require goals for each meeting as well.

4. **Debriefing reports.** Create a general Trade Show Debriefing Form *and* a Trade Show Meeting Summary, as follows:

- *Trade Show Debriefing Form:* Keep the form short and simple. Include Attendee name/title, trade show Date and Location, an Overview section (impressions of the event), Appointment Summary (total number of appointments plus names of each one), any General Notes, and Action Items (all follow-ups with dates). You can also consider a heading for Takeaways/Learnings.
- *Trade Show Meeting Summary:* Reps will complain about this, but it's essential that it be done for every appointment—including unscheduled ones. In a way, this should be regarded like any sales meeting report summary. It would include Attendees, Date/Time, Items Discussed, Action Items, and Takeaways/Learnings.

5. **Debriefing meeting.** This is where things can get interesting. The attendees would circulate their Debriefing Form and Trade Show

Meeting Summaries with the team (and possibly other teams and executives, if you think it would be of interest) in advance. The meeting would not be to read the forms, but rather to highlight the most important things from the event and then brainstorm about them as a team.

The debriefing meeting is a chance for your team members to shine and for you to mentor them. It's not about the "fun" of the event (assuming there was some had), but guiding them to understand how to build on what they observed and learned. In other words, it's not just about the details of the meetings and the action items—both of which are important, of course—but about what the attendees do with their newfound relationships.

For example, if one of your reps meets with an important buyer who had been elusive, this is a time to pounce. A follow-up e-mail is okay, but not enough. There should be a follow-up *phone call.* Or maybe it becomes an invitation for the buyer to visit your company's office. If the rep really hit it off with the buyer, maybe she can coordinate an in-person meeting at their office—or at some other mutually convenient location.

The secret is this: do not allow a hot lead to grow cold! Business cards get lost. Meeting discussions get forgotten. Opportunities that seemed exciting in the spur of the moment during a trade show suddenly fade into the background. Your reps need to be tenacious about these leads and build a sales community. You can't afford to allow a week to become a month or six months or a year later at the next trade show for your company to have another intersection with these people. And the way to engage the Millennial rep is to remind him or her that how she follows up is just as important to growing that community as the trade show meeting itself.

YOU NEVER KNOW WHO YOU'LL MEET

I heard a story about a company (let's call it ACME Jet Ski—because, why not?) that was on its last legs of attending a certain industry trade show. The show was a bummer for everyone: light attendance and little enthusiasm. The company had spent $100K to participate in the event—as they did each year—and had little to show for it. They certainly didn't get any sales or new business. The CEO mumbled to himself "Never again . . . never again. We're done."

The last day of the event dragged on. ACME attendees couldn't wait to take down the booth and head to the airport. They became so bored from inactivity that they started to shut down early. As a sales assistant stayed behind after the others and taped up the final box, a well-suited gentleman with a beard happened by and looked around curiously. His eyes switched from the Expo directory to all the barren booth walls that had formerly advertised ACME products. He paused to scratch his beard.

The sales assistant was anxious to scramble to the airport, but he couldn't leave this poor fellow in the lurch. "May I help you?"

"I'm looking for Kookamunga Jet Ski . . . do you know where their booth might be?"

"Oh, yes . . . my company bought them out a long time ago and re-branded their products." The sales assistant brightened, thankful that this might not be a total waste of time. He handed the man a business card and said "I'm Jeremy of ACME Jet Ski. How may I help you?"

"Well," the gentleman said. "My name is Hugo Ratcliffe."

"Pleased to meet you, Mr. Ratcliffe," Jeremy said, shaking his hand. "Are you a retailer?"

"I was in the business many years ago and left for other ventures. But now I've partnered with several other investors to create a new chain of recreational sports stores launching this fall. I used to love the skis made by Kookamunga . . . you say ACME continues to produce the same products under a new name?"

"Yes, we still produce all of them, in fact."

"That is fantastic news!" Mr. Radcliffe shouted, presenting his card. "I'm so glad I found you. I think we can do a lot of business together. I'm looking to start off with a purchase of about a hundred thousand jet skis . . . are you the person I should speak with?"

Jeremy thought he would go through the convention center's fifty-foot-high ceiling. *This deal could be worth millions*, he thought: *I'll finally be able to bring in my first new account!*

I admit I've changed the names of the people, the product, the companies, and the industry, but otherwise this story is true. Because the sales assistant was given the opportunity to attend the show—and happened to be the last person in his company still at the show—he ultimately landed a brand-new, multi-million-dollar account. Shortly thereafter, he was promoted.

Now, wasn't this fortuitous occurrence worth the expense of sending Jeremy to the trade show?

I've spent a lot of time in this chapter defining trade shows. If your industry does not have trade shows (or is truly dismissive of them, no matter what), there are many alternatives to help your team build a community and feel part of something much bigger—and the same techniques apply to all of them. Here are just a few:

- **Industry organizations and associations:** No doubt your industry has several. Encourage your employees to join (perhaps the company will be able to spring for membership fees). They should also be encouraged to attend events and become active in the organizations, as long as your company policies allow this.

- **Sales associations:** There are many sales associations that might be appropriate for them, depending on their job experience and level, including:

  - The American Association of Inside Sales Professionals (AA-ISP).
  - The National Association of Sales Professionals (NASDP). (This is an online community.)
  - The National Sales Network (NSN).
  - Sales and Marketing Executives International (SMEI).
  - The Sales Association.

- **Networking and public speaking organizations:** Toastmasters International not only helps train professionals at public speaking, it's also a great way to build a community. There are also many organizations, such as BNI, that help build referrals and networks. (As of this writing, BNI costs around $400 a year—which is a drop in the bucket if you consider the value of the network they can help create.)

■ **Alumni programs:** It doesn't matter where your employees went to college, every one of them has an alumni association. Usually they actively solicit attendees for networking events with special guest speakers.

At the end of the day, it doesn't matter how your team builds a sales community—as long as they do it. If you don't, your salespeople will become bored and stifled, whether they realize it or not. I would strongly recommend that they supplement their online (social media) groups with active participatory groups that have opportunities for face-to-face presentations and social gatherings. But again, the key is to make sure they recognize that every connection is an opportunity for a business relationship and, most importantly, *sales*!

5 Things to Remember

1. Offer your team members the opportunity to interact with real people in the flesh, not just online.
2. Consider sending young salespeople to industry trade shows to broaden their networks and improve their relationship skills.
3. Make sure attendees pre-plan attendance at the event with goals and scheduled appointments.
4. Ensure that attendees fill out Trade Show Debriefing Forms and Trade Show Meeting Summaries. (The latter is for every meeting.)
5. Consider these other community-building opportunities for your team: industry organizations and associations; networking and public-speaking organizations; and alumni programs.

•
•
•

CHAPTER TEN

APPLYING THE RIGHT PRESSURE WHILE APPRECIATING THEIR WORK/LIFE BALANCE

This may come as something of a shock to you. Most Millennials care more about job flexibility than they do about making big bucks or getting a huge promotion. That's not to say they don't care about salary increases or moving up the ladder; it's that personal freedom and space are *exceedingly important* to them.

Don't get me wrong: these people are putting in their work time. They just want to do it on their own terms and in their own way. While you may be the kind of person who wakes up at 6:00 a.m., showers, gets dressed, eats a hearty breakfast with the newspaper, commutes to work, and is at your desk doing business by 8:00 a.m., your team members are just not wired that way. They are probably *waking up* at 8:00 a.m. (if that early), texting, checking work e-mails, showering, texting, getting dressed, checking more business e-mails, texting, reading social-media posts, posting selfies, texting, commuting to work, stopping at Starbucks, texting during the wait for their lattes, answering business e-mails, and then strolling into work by 9:30 with cups in hand and backpacks on their shoulders.

You may give these employees the stink-eye as they appear through the door because you see them as *late and lazy*. I have news for you: they believe they already started their workdays at 8:00 a.m.—the same time as you! In fact, they never stop working: to them, it's all one continuous workday. They might have been answering work e-mails or texts until midnight or woke up to do so at 3:00 a.m. While you were fast asleep by 10:00 p.m. in la-la land heading toward your 6:00 a.m. buzzer, they were still going at it. Somewhere amidst all of the texting, posting, and e-mailing, *they believe they were doing work.* For them, the lines between work time and free time are blurred and not black-and-white the way you see them. Today's workforce is not in any way like the "clock-punching" employees of the past, which may be how you have been trained. These folks are texting and e-mailing all morning, throughout the day, well into the night, and early in the morning. Physical presence doesn't matter all that much.

The 9:00-to-5:00 job really doesn't exist as such for most people anymore. It's not a mystery why: *technology*. We can reach anyone and everyone 24/7 from pretty much anywhere a signal is available. The next generation of salespeople was raised with this mindset, so they are not hard-wired into feeling that they have to be in the office at a desk to be working. Company VPNs, videoconferencing, and dial-in phone conferences are the norm these days, which means your team doesn't feel the need to prove to you that they are "working."

Millennials do, however, need work environments that are casual and comfortable for them, which often means *wherever they happen to be*—Starbucks, a friend's couch, and perhaps even the john. If your company culture and HR rulebook don't accommodate flex schedules for your sales team, you are going to have a really hard time recruiting and retaining good young salespeople who have the potential to become stars. This is just an incontrovertible fact: your team believes they can do their jobs anywhere at virtually any time—and they need that flexibility to be able to mix things up in their workday as they see fit.

Sometimes companies cling to rigid, old-fashioned policies because they are worried that "other departments will be upset if your team comes and goes as they please." That's a ridiculous argument, in my opinion. I don't think clock-watching cultures work, and I certainly don't think the same rules from one team always apply to another. This is just the way it is: sales professionals *should be out of the office selling*. They can't pound the pavement for sales if they are chained to their desks. With all due respect to the folks in the warehouse who are working their butts off to pack and ship products, that job simply can't be done anywhere except at the warehouse, so in their case a rigid work schedule on-site is necessary to keep things moving and on track.

This is the fact: many large corporations, perhaps even yours, employ entire sales teams that have home offices. These salespeople hardly ever meet with their supervisors and co-workers in the flesh. They work their territories according to their own schedules. When their presence is needed—such as for a department or company meeting—they do so by phone conferences and videoconferences. Texting and IM (Instant Messaging) are starting to be used in companies as much as e-mail. Many companies have intranet sites and shared folders, so accessing important documents can be done in a snap.

If your company isn't ready for all that, fine. But again, you can't afford to not give salespeople *some* flexibility in their schedules. If the policy at your company restricts this, you might try writing a proposal to the executive team outlining all the proposed rules. You can even suggest doing it on a trial basis (e.g., 90 days) to test out if it will work. If your company doesn't have a flex policy and you are able to get one approved, you will come off as a hero to your team. This goes a long way toward earning their respect and trust.

In my view, these are the five most important ground rules:

1. **Establish "on hours":** These are the hours in which employees must be available by phone, video, e-mail, or text. If "on hours" are say, between 10:00 and 12:00 and/or 3:00 and 5:00, they'd better be answering the phone or e-mail, unless they have a scheduled appointment. If they are hung up with a call or truly preoccupied with business during the hours, the least they could do is e-mail or text back to say "I'm on a call with my buyer. Call you back in five."

2. **Establish a "calendar":** This could be a weekly, monthly, or annual in-office calendar, depending on your company's needs. Plan as far out in advance as possible when employees need to be in the office, so those days are blocked.

3. **Make it 100% clear that "on hours" and "the calendar" are subject to change.** This is not a lifetime arrangement or a contract. As the business changes, you may need to adjust #1 or #2—and employees can't be upset about it. If you need an employee in the office on a certain day at a specific time, that person had better be able to show up as needed.

   You also reserve the right to do a "bed check" every so often. It's not that you don't trust your people—well, some you do, some you don't—but you can't afford to have people spending work time getting paid to goof around or interview with other companies. Your bed check should be a friendly call in which you are asking how the employee is faring on various tasks and determining if he or she needs your help or support on anything. By doing this, you are demonstrating that you care about them and what they do—which will be appreciated. Chances are, they do have some questions and issues that could benefit from your wisdom.

4. **The work must get done:** If an employee is not getting tasks done on time, you need to give some warnings that the flex arrangement is at risk.

5. **The sales targets must be met:** If the employee is not able to produce enough unit sales and target revenue, there is probably a bigger issue going on. Still, the flex schedule might need to change for an employee who isn't carrying his or her weight.

There are other factors here as well. As you've probably picked up by now, Millennials need *play and/or relaxation* time—or at least the sense that their jobs enable them to feel like they can unwind in some fashion. Some will want/expect to use lunch hours and/or breaks to go to the gym, do yoga or t'ai chi, meditate, and so on. This is okay in my book, as long as the above five rules are followed. I've heard stories about employees who were late for (or even missed) scheduled meetings—video, phone, and in-person—because they were at a yoga class. Really? Well, that won't fly—*ever*. If/when this occurs, you need to hold employees accountable: If they don't follow the rules, then the flex privileges go bye-bye.

If an employee has good communication skills—phone and e-mail— and is responsive, you should be able to accommodate his or her need for "balance." The downside is that the folks who work in the office and don't need flex hours or "balance" may feel gypped, alone, or that the team lacks cohesion and camaraderie. There may not be enough opportunities to share experiences, techniques, and tricks for the team to benefit each other. From my perspective, you want the experienced salespeople to pass along their wisdom to the younger reps as much as possible. With so many team members being spread out off-site and others working flex hours, this is a significant challenge for any sales leader. It's ironic that the same folks who require work/life balance and flex hours also crave community and team spirit—and they are counting on you, as the leader, to provide these things for them.

In number three above, I wrote that "on hours" and the "calendar" are subject to change. This means that, any time you feel the team needs a unifying boost, you should plan an event in the office (or out of the office) with all team members (non-negotiable). This can be difficult to coordinate, but it can be helpful for everyone.

THE ON-SITE VS. OFF-SITE DILEMMA

Working from home is a *privilege* for employees. Sure, the companies save some money on office space and such for these individuals, but it's still a privilege because the employees are getting paid to do their jobs with minimal supervision. Off-site people have a great deal of personal freedom. The company doesn't know if the employee is really putting in a full eight hours of work each day or is spending that time interviewing with other companies, freelancing, writing their novels, doing personal chores, exercising, binge-eating, social-media posting, Internet surfing, playing electronic games, goofing around with their dogs, or just napping the day away. Companies need to have a great deal of trust when it comes to off-site employees, and the folks who do work in the office are obviously under much closer scrutiny than their off-site brethren.

There are major downsides for off-site employees, too. True, they don't have a boss breathing down their necks all day. But they also often can't get hold of their bosses when they really need them for a decision. If they don't get a call back or response to an urgent e-mail, off-site employees can easily get frustrated and paranoid: "Why isn't she getting back to me? It's been an *hour* already. I wrote that it was *urgent.* Maybe she blames me for the problem and thinks I screwed up. Maybe I'm being fired!"

Of course, the manager in the aforementioned scenario could have been called into a spur-of-the-moment meeting with her boss. Or maybe there was a fire drill. Or maybe mustard got on her business suit and she scurried into the rest room to scrub it off. Who knows? If the off-site employee had been on site, it would have been a simple hallway question to a co-worker: "Hey, do you know where Martha went?"

I'm not suggesting you have sympathy for the off-site folks—just a little understanding that they do miss out on direct communication with their bosses and co-workers and often miss crucial pieces of hallway conversation that would have made their jobs easier.

For in-person gatherings, delegate some assignments (e.g., leading a session) to team members—especially the people who are hardly around. This is an opportunity for them to be seen and heard. If you handle this correctly, everyone will feel like he or she is part of the team and contributing to the same effort.

Your role in this setting is to remind the team about goals and targets, allow everyone to participate, keep everyone focused, and bring challenges out in the open while everyone is present. You may only need to do this group session once a quarter or even once a year and can time it to coincide with other events (such as a corporate meeting or sales conference)—but it is important to carve out time for bonding. You may even find it beneficial for the entire group to let loose together for drinks after hours—or you could do something more planned, such as taking them to a comedy show or a basketball game.

Better yet: if you are really brave and want to show off how "open" you are to new ideas and "balance," you might even suggest having the group attend a yoga or t'ai chi class together if that's something you know team members are into. It will go a long way to show you are "one of the team" and a good sport.

5 Things to Remember

1. Work/life balance is critical for Millennials.
2. You need to hire and retain the best people possible, so accommodate work/life balance requests the best you can—even if they impose on you and involve overcoming interdepartmental office politics.
3. Millennials work 24/7 and don't require an office environment to feel like they are working.

4. If you are able to offer flex and/or off-site privileges to employees, make certain they follow the ground rules at all times—especially being "on call" and adhering to the "calendar."
5. Like it or not, in order to build a cohesive team when you have a mix of people on-site, off-site, and doing flex hours, you will need to work harder and take extra steps for community building.

•
•
•

CHAPTER ELEVEN

LEADING BY EXAMPLE

As someone who oversees a sales organization or team, you probably consider yourself to be a good leader and a strong role model. But what does this really mean to today's sales professionals?

They won't tell you this directly, but they expect you to *walk the walk and talk the talk at all times.* They have low tolerance for what they regard as "unethical behavior" of any kind, which may sometimes call into question where you are accustomed to drawing the line. The problem is that they won't tell you what their moral line is or where it is drawn; they expect that you *already know all this.* If you fail in their eyes in this regard, they probably won't tell you, since they assume that you would do the upstanding thing and admit it. Even then, they might not forgive you because you have fallen so far and they have already spoken to their work friends about it—if not also to your boss and to the HR director.

There is a great line in the Alfred Hitchcock film *North by Northwest* in which advertising executive Roger Thornhill (played by Cary Grant) is accused of "lying" by his secretary (yes, that was the title back then). His answer: "It's not lying; it's an expedient exaggeration of the truth."

LIAR, LIAR, PANTS ON FIRE

A good salesperson doesn't tell an all-out lie—and should never have to. If she does, it means they don't understand the product or services and they certainly aren't adhering to company policies (assuming the company is an upstanding organization). Or the salesperson is a pathological liar—which might work *sometimes*. But it only takes one time for even the most adept pathological liar to get exposed, which means lost customers and permanent damage to the company's reputation.

If Millennials figure out that you or anyone on your team is unethical in any fashion, they will head in the opposite direction and work someplace else. That said, there are tiny gray areas where companies may need to look the other way. This is where it gets challenging for sales leaders, who must explain—and perhaps even defend—these positions to the best of their ability. The best you can do in these gray situations is to *listen* to these concerns and try to address them the best you can—first and foremost, by asking your team members for suggestions on alternate ways of tackling them.

Sales is sometimes like that. We say what we have to say to make the sale—up to a point, at least (certainly not encroaching on anything of a legal nature). The "expedient exaggeration of the truth" or LWL ("Little White Lie") is part of the game. The buyers know this. *Everyone* knows this. Your company's product is *always* going to be better than the competition, even if it's not. A pharmaceutical rep is always going to downplay the side effects of a new wonder drug as "extremely rare" and cite the case-study stats. What dummy salesperson is going to say otherwise?

But here are examples of the types of sticky ethical situations Millennial salespeople must grapple with:

1. During a phone conference, a buyer insists upon the product arriving in their warehouse by April 1 or the deal is completely off. The previous day, the VP of Operations had openly said in a meeting: "There's no way in hell it's getting there before April 15."

   The sales leader's answer to the buyer on the phone: "No problem. We'll make it."

2. A Millennial rep tells his sales leader that the team's #1 salesperson wrote an inappropriate e-mail (it had an off-putting tone—not of a harassment nature) to someone in another division of the company.

The sales leader's answer to the employee: "Thank you for letting me know. I'll dig into it."

3. A young salesperson gets a total skip on a product from a key buyer. In a panic, he calls his sales leader from the parking lot and asks "What should I do?"

The sales leader tells his rep: "Go back in there right now and say that you can't accept anything less than 1,000 units. Tell her you'll get fired without the order."

All three of the aforementioned scenarios actually occurred (with different people and in different companies). Guess what: in each of the three situations, the sales manager was "right" to varying degrees.

1. After the meeting with the buyer, the sales leader who "lied" shoots straight toward the office of the VP of Operations and begs him to shave off two weeks of production time so they can make the buyer's deadline. They work together and figure out how to make it happen.

2. The sales leader follows up as promised, and it turns out the rep was correct: the e-mail had an inappropriate tone. The sales leader gives the (former) #1 salesperson a severe verbal and written warning and instructs him to apologize to the recipient. An e-mail is sent to HR documenting the incident, along with evidence. The sales leader also personally calls the person on the receiving end of the offensive e-mail and apologizes on behalf of his employee.

3. The rep goes from the parking lot back to his buyer's office. He tells the buyer the sad story that he needs the order or else he'll lose his job. The buyer feels bad and purchases the target quantity.

All of the above scenarios ended the way they should, right? Not exactly. In each circumstance, the Millennial rep saw his supervisor as a *bad leader*. Huh? But doesn't the result matter most? Well, let's take another look at each scenario from the rep's perspective:

1. The only thing that sticks in the mind of the rep is the false date given to the buyer. It doesn't matter that the sales leader knows from experience that he can finesse the schedule with the VP of Operations and make it work after the fact. He is going against a specific statement made by the VP of Operations.

2. The rep assumes the sales leader has let the #1 salesperson "get away with bad behavior." He goes to colleagues and HR to complain about the sales leader "playing favorites." He has no idea that behind the scenes, the sales leader is holding that person accountable for his inappropriate behavior and that he smoothed over the situation with the offended party.

3. The rep receives the order (possibly), but feels that either: a) His job would have been truly in jeopardy if he failed, or b) The sales leader lied to him about firing him to get the order. Whichever was the case, he doesn't care whether the tactic worked: he feels manipulated (and he is right).

   And what happens if the order *doesn't* come in from this tactic? Would you, as the supervisor, really fire him?

Millennials are ingrained with their own special ethical codes, and they expect you to recognize and share them. They are salespeople, but their ethical standards outweigh the need to close deals. They would rather walk away than make any compromise to their beliefs. They also believe that they should be told the *who, what, where, how,* and *why* of everything. Yes, it seems like babying to have to go through all this with each and every circumstance, but this is what the sales leader needed to do in each circumstance with his rep:

1. After the phone conference with the buyer, the sales leader needed to pull the rep aside and explain "the lie." He could have said something like: "I've known John [the VP of Operations] for years. He always pads the schedule. Let's go chat with him together and explain the situation. I guarantee it'll work; you'll see."

2. This situation is especially sticky because what happens between the sales leader and the guilty #1 salesperson should be treated as confidential between manager and direct report. But the

Millennial rep needs to *see* that the individual was held accountable and that justice was served. He may even have expected that the person should have been fired (though of course it's not up to him). In the next 1:1 meeting with the young rep, the sales leader needs to say: "Thank you for bringing that situation to my attention before it really blew up. I took care of it confidentially, which is out of respect to all parties—including you." When presented in this fashion, the rep will appreciate that he was kept in the loop and protected, and the time was taken to provide an update and explanation.

3. During the phone call in the parking lot, the sales leader should just say outright: "We really need this order or we'll fall behind on our revenue budget and there will be hell to pay. Go back inside to the buyer and find out *why* it was declined—you *deserve* a reason. Have a conversation. Ask questions. Once you know the *why*, you can present an answer to the objection with a response that solves his problem and fits his need." I guarantee the buyer will admire the rep's *chutzpah* coming back inside—not to push the sale, mind you, but to ask *why*.

    Three things happen: 1. The conversation leads to trust. 2. The questions he asks lead to identifying the buyer's *need*. 3. The rep answers the *need* with a specific problem-solving *benefit* of the product. The buyer may now be on the fence about placing an order, but this is the opportunity for the rep to suggest a "trial run" of a small quantity to start. This is much better than a manipulative, unethical move that may backfire—or a total skip, right?

Recognize that it doesn't take much for Millennials to judge every move you make based on their own moral compass—whether they know the facts or not. The point is, they feel they are entitled to *know* the facts even when they aren't. But if you are able to bring them in the loop and explain things to them, perhaps they will learn how the game is played and will see that you are always 110% honest and transparent with them and with your company and would *never* do anything that is below-board with your customers. The key is to make sure they understand where your moral compass points and where you draw your line.

"Walking the walk and talking the talk" is vital to anyone managing Millennials today. You can't hold employees accountable to follow company policies and professional cultural standards if you don't do the same at all times yourself. As the leader of a sales organization, you must be aware that your team is constantly analyzing, interpreting, and judging everything you say, do, and write. They will not tell you directly when their moral compass flashes red lights that tell them that you've crossed the line: their expectation is that you are the leader and you should already know not to step past it. You are the "adult"—i.e., "parent"—and should always inherently set the example. But note that they will have no issue telling others—co-workers, your supervisor, or HR—when they feel uncomfortable with something you said, did, or wrote. It may have been taken out of context or completely misinterpreted, but it doesn't get you off the hook. I know an executive who once said to a sales leader: "If you fart in your office, team members three floors below will smell it." It's crass, but it's the absolute truth!

It is more difficult to earn the trust and confidence of Millennials than other generations—but, once you do, they will be loyal and stand by your side forever.

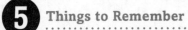

5 **Things to Remember**

1. Always "walk the walk and talk the talk" when it comes to setting an ethical standard for your team.
2. Millennials have a strong ethical sense, but they won't tell you where they draw the line.
3. When you are facing murky, gray areas of "truth-telling" in sales, over-explain your strategy to your team upfront and have them help you come up with alternate solutions if they don't buy into yours.
4. Be transparent with your team at all times; if you aren't, it becomes nearly impossible to earn their trust.
5. Recognize that your Millennial reps are judging you as much on your ethics as they are on your ability to lead and direct the team.

:

CHAPTER TWELVE

TEACHING WITHOUT PREACHING

If your team ever feels like you are lecturing or preaching to them, they will tune you out. They may even mimic you and laugh at you behind your back. If you are the type who enjoys telling stories of the "old days," watch out—then they are going to heckle and rib you right to your face. Trust me when I say they don't want to hear any of your old sales war dog stories.

Deep down, today's salespeople believe they know and understand more than you do (and ever will). They are also confident that they can find out whatever they don't know in a heartbeat with a Google search. There is some truth to the latter; they are incredibly facile when it comes to finding out stuff on the Internet.

SOMETIMES THE OLD DOGS DON'T WANT TO LEARN NEW TRICKS

You should always be receptive to learning from your team as well. When you pick up on something from a young team member, make sure to give her ample thanks and praise.

As for your senior salespeople, recognize that they won't be all that happy if it comes across that you are overtly pandering to the young people and spending a lot of meeting time teaching them things that are second-nature to the senior folks. On the flip side, Millennials may not be all that tolerant if your senior folks don't "get" technical stuff or refuse to adapt and move on when it's obvious to everyone else that a change needs to happen.

I knew of an accomplished senior rep who had been selling from printed brochures and catalogs for forty years. When a corporate decision was made to stop printing the brochures and catalogs because they were all available digitally, he refused to accept the decision and kept pressing Marketing to make catalogs—*just for him*. He claimed that his accounts were old-fashioned and wouldn't even look at the online catalog. His accounts made up roughly 3% of the company's overall revenue, but the cost of printing the catalog just for him would have eaten up all the profits from his sales.

As it turned out, this was a case of the rep being *accustomed* to selling from print brochures and catalogs. He was using the preferences of his accounts as an excuse and a cop-out. Needless to say, this didn't fly. The team rallied to his side by "teaching" him the benefits of the online catalog. On the plus side, they showed him that corrections and updates can be made in real-time online, as opposed to a printed catalog, which is forever. One Millennial rep had even created a beautiful format that was perfect for an iPad presentation.

In the hands of a good salesperson, there is no difference between a paper catalog and the same catalog on an iPad. Well, actually, the latter is *much better*, which the rep finally came to realize—thanks to his Millennial teammates.

The problem, of course, is that they don't know what they don't know and they accept a lot of what they find from Google searching as pure fact. Once they find "an answer," they probably think they are "all done" and don't have to dig any further.

It's not easy teaching people who think they know everything and have the universe right at their fingertips. Ironically, as covered in Chapter Four, Millennials love training—and always think they need more of it. They probably just don't want it coming from you. (Don't take offense at this; it's like hearing advice from a parent.) Even so, you are the sales leader, and there will most certainly be moments when you will need to teach your reps *something*. And you'll have to do it in such a way that they don't feel like it's an actual lesson. If you do, they will phase right out and sneak peaks at their phones every two seconds.

If you want to instruct your team on something that doesn't require full training, here are some tips:

1. **Make it lightning fast!:** They have really short attention spans. Start off right away by saying "This will only take five minutes"—and then *only take five minutes.*

2. **Avoid stories from your past:** No matter how good the story might be, they will think you are a boring old fart. Instead, tell a quick joke— but it better be funny (and inoffensive).

3. **Provide the *who, what, when, where, and why:*** In condensed fashion (remember: I just said it needs to be lightning fast!), offer some context for what you are about to tell them. If they know *why* you are talking about it ("this method raised sales in the other division 10% year over year"), they'll become more vested in it.

4. **Make it super casual:**
   - No PowerPoint.
   - No handouts.
   - Jot down your main points on the whiteboard as you say them.
   - Avoid any corporate-speak whatsoever.

5. **Make it participatory and fun:**
   - Turn it into an "interactive" lesson—they are on their computers and can click on things and show you how smart they are.
   - Make it a game, if you can. Even a guessing game or trivia game is better than you standing there as a talking head.
   - Brainstorm—let them teach themselves and each other.

Another way to go about this is to bring in a guest from another part of the company to share your "lesson" with your team. No offense to you, but in all likelihood your group will be more respectful to a popular leader from a different department who is an expert on the subject. If this is the case, share in advance with your guest what you would like to see achieved. Make sure to run through all of the instructions I provide in this chapter. The worst thing that could happen is that you bring in a team leader who tells her boring stories or does a PowerPoint. You could have put them to sleep all on your own without soliciting her help.

Better yet, if you could avoid "teaching" in a 1:1 meeting or team meeting, that's even better. How do you do it? Create *teachable moments*—but without anyone necessarily having made a mistake. In other words, in front of your "pupil," demonstrate the "lesson" in real time with the buyer present or with a more seasoned rep. After the teachable moment happens, don't preach. All you need to ask is "Did you catch that? Any questions?" If your student says "Yes" and then "No," respectively, to these questions, follow up with: "So, you are good doing something like that?"

Nine out of ten times, the Millennial rep will pick up on the teachable moment and appreciate it far more than time spent in a boring discussion or meeting. If she's enthusiastic and replies "Yeah—that was great! Really useful," then you would come back with "Terrific. Give it a try and tell me how it works out."

If it's the oddball tenth time (and maybe the rep is slower on the take) and she says "I think I need a little training on that," then explain it further during a 1:1 session. Don't waste time on the lesson with the entire group, even though there may be others who also didn't get it. If you provided the teachable moment and they didn't ask for more explanation or help, it's up to them to sink or swim.

5 **Things to Remember**

. . . .

1. Never tell your team stories of the "old days" of sales. They hate them.
2. Recognize that you still have to teach Millennials on occasion—even when they think they know everything.
3. Be careful to avoid seeming to pander to Millennials who are needier than your other team members.
4. Make any and all instruction quick, participatory, and fun.
5. Wherever possible, try to create "teachable moments" on the fly—even if a mistake hasn't been made. Everyone will appreciate that you saved the team boring meeting time.

CHAPTER THIRTEEN

•
•
○

CONDUCTING TEAM MEETINGS

For most companies, meetings are a necessary evil. You can't avoid them. As has been mentioned in earlier chapters, meetings have changed dramatically over the years—but to many people it doesn't mean that they have become any less painful. Mainly, phone conferences and videoconferences have become the norm. During the latter, people can type in "chats" (quick text messages) to individuals or the whole group rather than having to fight to get a word in edgewise. (Often the message is this: "We can't hear you—speak louder!")

As a sales leader, you no doubt attend a ton of meetings and run many of them. You've probably spent hundreds of days when you can't recall having accomplished a single thing because you've been stuck in meetings. If you hate them, imagine how your team feels. Today's salespeople are easily bored, restless, and impatient and probably hate meetings as much as you do, though for different reasons.

On the other hand, remember that Millennials crave *community* and love *collaboration.* If they enjoy brainstorming and thrive on picking each other's brains, they might look forward to some meetings. On the surface, this isn't a bad thing. But there are people out there who are social butterflies and want to be part of *absolutely everything*—even if it has nothing to do with sales. That might sound nice and produce Kumbaya bonding moments, but they will distract your team members and prevent them from doing what they are paid to do: *sell!*

I can't stress the importance of this enough. If you have salespeople spending all their time at meetings, they aren't out there pounding the pavement for sales. They aren't getting to know their customers, they aren't upselling, and they aren't creating new accounts. It may sound harsh, but if you get a whiff that one of your salespeople is flitting from one meeting to the next when he needs to be out selling, read him the riot act.

If you have any measure of control over your team's meeting schedule, what do you think is the first thing you need to do? No, it's not a trick question. Here's the simple answer: cancel as many meetings as you possibly can. Neither you nor your team members need to attend every meeting. Their role is to sell. Your role is to *maximize revenue, build the business, and lead/mentor the team.* You don't have time to sit in meetings all day. If you can eradicate some meetings for your team, a few of them may want to build a statue of you in the parking lot. (Well, maybe not . . . but they will be forever grateful—for about a week.)

For those meetings you *do* retain, whittle down the time spent in them—*by half.* An hour meeting should be a half hour. A half-hour meeting should be fifteen minutes. A fifteen-minute meeting should be . . . five minutes. No, my math isn't wrong. There's no such thing as a seven and a half-minute meeting, so shave off an extra two and a half minutes.

Here's another time-saver: If you really feel you need to schedule the meeting room for an hour *just in case,* that's fine. But if the meeting only needs to be thirty minutes, then do the unimaginable: *end it early!* Don't try to extend it to an hour just because you have the room for an hour or the meeting invite says it's an hour. I believe that meetings always end up going at the pace of the scheduled meeting request, rather than taking the amount of time that is actually needed. People stretch out meetings all the time—they like the people in the room, they need a break from computer work, or they're avoiding doing something—so call them out on it as necessary. It's a simple equation that requires zero knowledge of math:

$$time = sales = money$$

Create an agenda in advance for every meeting to avoid wasted time within the meeting figuring out what needs to be discussed. If you don't have a full enough agenda for a standing weekly or monthly meeting, guess what you should do: cancel it! People love being given back a half hour or hour of their time. To some people, it's as good as finding a twenty-dollar bill on the ground.

When you are creating the agenda, boil your items down to only the things you need to review as a team. (Keep training sessions separate, if you can, to maintain focus.) Make sure to include areas of opportunity in which every team member can participate. Send the agenda to everyone in advance of the meeting, so they know what's coming and can prepare for it. Solicit suggestions for agenda items from the team—but only add them if you have time. If not, save them for another time and day.

For meetings you run, keep the agenda airtight. You are the moderator and are responsible for running it in an orderly fashion. Don't allow anyone to "hog" meeting time or derail the schedule. You are well within your rights to reel things back in. Acknowledge that the issue is important, but then politely put it in the "parking lot" for a later meeting. (If you say this, make sure you *remember to follow through and do it*: Millennials especially look to you to be a person of his or her word.)

Wherever possible, keep your team *engaged*. A brief product demo—especially a video on a big screen—can be fun. Anything that smacks of digital or technology (except PowerPoint!) would be terrific, as long as you understand how to run it. If you fumble with an app, for example, your lack of tech knowledge will be exposed and your team may look down on you for wasting their time.

During the meeting, share wins and positive news with the team, and single out any standout accomplishments. Your team will thrive when they feel they are being noticed and appreciated in front of their peers. Caveat: be careful to avoid seeming like you are playing favorites, as this will backfire. Always back up praise for someone with specific data points and examples. You do not have to praise everyone all the time, however. Your Millennials may have grown up in an era in which everyone in the kids' soccer league received a trophy, but in the real world honor and glory must be earned by *doing things above and beyond the norm*. How do they get rewarded for doing the day-to-day? A paycheck!

Aside from dragging meeting length, what do you think is the biggest killer of meetings? *Poor communication*. In this case, I don't mean bad public speakers (although I'm sure there are plenty), but poor communication caused by technology. Millennials love gizmos and, as mentioned, phone and videoconferencing services can be excellent tools. But every company knows what I'm talking about when I say that technology fails more than it succeeds during meetings. This can be especially painful when there are a lot of people who attend a meeting from off-site.

I've heard all kinds of stories from people about the problems that can arise when people are on the other side of phone or video conferences. During phone conference meetings, you can hear all kinds of horrific, distracting things going on: dogs barking, vacuum cleaners humming, kids screaming, etc. In spite of all the technology at our fingertips, connections can still have a lot of static and *really suck*. People get disconnected mid-sentence. Voices sound garbled, video images freeze up (with facial expressions contorted), employees talk over each other, people in the meeting room shuffle papers and rustle their lunch bags, speakerphones don't reach far enough, people show up late or have to leave early, and on and on. Then there are the dopes who can't get a word into the conversation because they've been on mute for ten minutes.

It's a wonder any work at all gets done at these meetings!

THAT MEETING WAS PRETTY DOPE—BUT DON'T BE ONE

There is a school of thought that companies need to adapt to Millennial-speak. Eventually, that will all come to pass as the Millennial generation continues to move up the ladder. I'm sure you've already heard enough foreign Millennial words in your office to fill a dictionary.

If you are moderating a meeting, avoid using Millennial jargon—or do so at your own peril. You could be saying the word or phrase completely wrong. It's not just pronunciation and meaning, there are potentially some contextual issues and body language involved. If you are a hair off—or end up choosing a word that is more "gangsta" than you intended—you could look pretty stupid, if not even get yourself into trouble.

Never try to be hip, cool, dope, or chill. You are a *sales leader*. You don't need to "prove" you are from their generation or are hooked into it (maybe because you have Millennial offspring of your own). If you try to

> tell a Millennial-type joke and it misfires, your team will think you are
> a fool and are trying too hard. You will be embarrassed. On the extreme
> side, your ignorance on language could cause you to be called into
> HR or your boss's office. Some Millennials have extra sensitivities on
> race, gender, religion, sexuality, equality, nationality, politics, human
> rights—and even seemingly innocuous things like sports, music, and
> books—so choose your words carefully at all times (a smart idea in all
> business situations anyway, from HR and legal standpoints).
>
> Be yourself—and be careful. In this day and age, people misconstrue
> and misinterpret things all the time, and you can't take any chances
> while trying to impress and win over your team.
>
> Don't say I didn't warn you!

Some of these problems are preventable, while others are not. I've always found that if a videoconference isn't working for someone—their computer may not sustain the most current version of Facetime, for example—go straight to phone conferencing. If a phone conference sounds like crap, have everyone dial in all over again—*right away*. If that still doesn't work, try a different phone conferencing line or service entirely. If it's not working after ten minutes, *call it quits and reschedule!* Do not waste your time fumbling with technology that will continue to derail you. Move on! Your team will be praising their maker for your decision. Nothing is more frustrating than when the communication technology is subpar.

When you have a mix of on-site and off-site team members, I have found that establishing ground rules and adhering to them are of the utmost importance:

1. **For the moderator:** Start on time! Unless a client is attending, do not wait for all attendees to start. If a person comes in late, don't waste time starting up a conversation with the person, just keep right on trucking. And do not repeat what was already said for anyone—including your boss—except a client. It's super annoying for the people who already heard these points and often opens up new discussions and problems, creating meeting churn.

2. **For the moderator:** Don't talk too much! This is a big pitfall for all leaders, not just sales leaders. They love a captive audience and

relish hearing their own voices. You will be far more effective if you speak less and in sound bites.

3. **For people in the meeting room:** Keep whispers and side conversations to a minimum. Try not to shuffle papers or make noise with your food and wrappers if it's a lunch meeting. Assume the people on the phone are trying to listen intently to each individual speaker.

4. **For remote-working people on the phone or video lines:** Find a private place to have the conversation, away from the barking dogs and screaming children. Try not to be in a noisy public place (such as a New York City street or in a coffee shop) for the call. If it can't be avoided, use the mute button when you are not speaking to avoid background noise. (But then remember to press the button again when you do speak!)

5. **For the moderator:** Be aware that you have an important task—keeping the meeting going and making sure everyone is heard. You need to stop all side conversations. You also need to be the one to repeat what has been said in the room or on the phone to be sure everyone has been properly understood. The person on the phone will be thankful you did this; it shows you have been engaged in what she's said, and it gives her an opportunity to correct or elaborate on anything that might have been misheard or misinterpreted.

6. **For attendees:** Speak loudly and clearly so people on the phone can hear and understand you. Keep your statements concise, and avoid jokes that could be misinterpreted by people on the phone. (Remember: they can't see your facial expressions and body language.) When you aren't speaking to the group, keep your mouth shut. No side conversations. Do not rustle papers, whistle, tap your feet, or chomp on potato chips. You don't want to be the person singled out as the distraction!

There are a lot of things you can control with your team—and a lot of things you can't. The pace and tone of your meetings is something that you *can control*. If you make your meetings short, productive, and engaging and build a community with team spirit, you will gain everyone's trust, and people will look forward to attending.

5 **Things to Remember**

1. Cut out nonessential meeting attendance for both yourself and your team.
2. Shave half the time off standing meetings.
3. Stick rigidly to meeting times. End early if you can, and give the time back to your team to sell stuff.
4. Use technology to engage your team, as long as you are 100% certain that the device or software will function properly.
5. Follow my meeting ground rules and adhere to them—especially when it comes to communicating with off-site personnel.

•
•
•

CHAPTER FOURTEEN

COMMUNICATING ON A REGULAR BASIS

Everyday communication is where things can get really hairy. You may think you've completely laid things out for one of your fresh young recruits. You've trained him, you've offered reminders at department meetings, you've provided coaching in 1:1 sessions, and you've sent follow-up e-mails.

Six weeks go by, and all is quiet. No news is good news, right?

Well, guess what: your sales "dude" has been stuck at the starting gate for the entire six weeks. In your view, he's done absolutely nothing proactive to move the needle. Is this fresh young sales "dude" recruit a "dud"? Or is something else happening here?

There are some sales reps who become deer in the headlights and freeze up. There are also others who are no doubt just plain duds. But then there are those who are stuck in the "Millennial validation mode" and need constant communication and reassurance from you to "*Go!*" (whatever the task might be—but especially *selling*). Whatever you seem to try to do to get things going, the training wheels won't come off the bike.

When you started in sales, you were probably a bull charging out of the gate. You didn't know who was riding on your back or whom you were charging at. In fact, at first you probably had no idea what you were doing at all. You didn't know anything or anyone, and you didn't care one iota. Ignorance was bliss, right? You couldn't wait to make some monster sales and prove your worth. You probably BS'd your way through your first pitches, busted your butt, and broke a few records—maybe even pissed off a few people along the way and apologized later. You were one fire-breathing hell-on-wheels sales machine! You couldn't wait to come back to the office for a hero's welcome, some pats on the back, and a hefty commission check.

Over the years, once you became a sales leader, you worked with and trained the superstars, as well as the good, the bad, and the ugly. Some were natural-born salespeople with fires in their bellies, whereas others needed an occasional kick in the rump to get jump-started.

But the Millennials are an entirely different breed. During those six stagnant weeks (or however long it is), your rep was waiting for you to scream "*Go! Sell! Do it!*" You are positive you already gave the go-ahead with flashing neon lights—*multiple times*. But trust me when I say that it wasn't nearly enough for them.

Once Millennials are out of college and surviving on their own (although some may indeed still be living at home), they don't quite get the idea that the "training wheels are off." They are frightened of the real world and the workplace. Mostly, they are afraid of failure and of disappointing you. What they don't realize is that inaction is probably the *only* way they could fail and disappoint you.

Young sales professionals are not accustomed to having doors slammed on their noses and don't understand that the nature of the job is being on the receiving end of rejection. They are going to make mistakes and fail. They can do everything right and *still fail*, which is part of the sales learning process.

STUCK IN FIRST GEAR

One of my clients told me about a talented 22-year-old rep—let's call him Richard—who seemed determined to make big sales. He was smart and aggressive. No one had any doubt he'd be off and running in the first week.

Unfortunately, he didn't do anything the first week, the second week . . . or the third. Other reps with much lesser presentation skills were piling on the sales, but Richard remained stuck in first gear.

When grilled about what was wrong, he could hardly explain himself. He knew the product. He had his pitch down pat. In training sessions he fielded objections better than anyone.

Finally, in a roundabout way, Richard admitted to his boss: "I can't explain it. It just feels weird. . . . It's like I'm *not ready*. I feel like I'm still at the kid's table or something."

Aha! Finally, the answer had emerged.

Now, as it happened, the sales leader knew that Richard was a big baseball fan and had even expressed some interest in playing for the company's softball team. The sales leader asked Richard if he had ever seen the film *Bull Durham* starring Kevin Costner.

"Of course—I love that movie!" Richard roared back.

"Remember the line 'Don't *think* . . . it can only hurt the ballclub'?"

"Yeah," Richard laughed. "That was hilarious."

"Sales is a lot like baseball. *Don't think: just do.* Eventually, every professional ballplayer making his debut in the major leagues has to throw that scary first pitch. Well, Richard. You're all warmed up and on the mound. Show us your stuff."

"I never thought of it that way," Richard considered.

"Welcome to the adults' table."

In these cases, managers have been known to try one or both extremes: hands-off (sink or swim) or micromanaging. Neither one of these approaches will work. The former will obviously cause stagnation, whereas the latter will offend these employees and they will: a) hate you; b) continue to underperform; and c) quit or get fired. Then you have to start the entire recruiting/replacement process all over again and face yet another Millennial, who will probably have the same exact problems getting started.

Your role, as leader/manager and coach, is to provide as much reassurance and confidence as needed by your team members. I know—it's a pain. You personally didn't require all this back-and-forth, nor did the myriad Boomer and Gen-X reps you've trained over the years. But you can't have your whole team stuck, either.

Here's what you need to do:

1. **Train, train, train:** After the training, force them to say outright that they "*get it*." Ask them to repeat back what they need to do and the exact sales pitches.

2. **Go, go, go!:** Tell them "Go!" verbally in 1:1 sessions, in meetings, in hallway conversations, and everywhere else. There should be no doubt whatsoever in their minds that you have given the "Go!" signal. If the rep looks puzzled as if she's hearing it for the first time, say "Go!" once again, loud and clear.

3. **Coach, coach, coach:** At each and every opportunity—1:1 meetings and even during hallway conversations—stop to specifically ask: "How's it going? Did you get started? Any sales objections?" Pay attention to body language. If he is hesitating or looking away, this is a flashing red light. Press further. If he is struggling with something, spend extra time to find out what is holding him back. If a rep says to you: "I didn't know we were supposed to 'go.' I don't feel like I'm ready," then ask what he isn't "ready for" after all the training. Clearly end the conversation by saying that you will be checking in on his progress at the next 1:1 session.

4. **Praise, praise, praise:** If a stuck team member gets unstuck, lavish the praise and reward the behavior. Encourage *more* of it. Do not fault the rep if she misses the mark or didn't get the sale. All you need to do is say "Great work—keep at it. If you keep charging after sales, eventually you'll get the hang of it and something will break through. I have confidence in you."

5. **Collaborate, collaborate, collaborate:** If fear of failure continues to be an issue, have team members offer a pointer or two. Most of the time, it's just a matter of one team member helping another get into the right mindset. Sometimes hearing the same thing you've said from a peer is what sparks the action. At the end of the day, it doesn't matter if the push came from you or someone else. The important thing is that the sales rep is working toward making the sale.

In case you haven't deduced it by now, you need to take on the communication style of *over-communicating*. This doesn't in any way mean telling your team what to do all the time or how to do it. Micromanaging, barking orders, and/or being hypercritical will, in fact, have the opposite effect and *demotivate* your team. I also don't suggest over-explaining or stating the obvious; your people aren't stupid.

By stressing that you over-communicate with your team, I mean that you must have frequent interaction by constantly being engaged with every member. On a regular basis you must communicate with your team in person (for on-site people), on the phone, in videoconferences, and via e-mail—period. In other words, never assume that your Millennial team members are up and running. Even if they seem well prepared and say nothing to you (or "everything's great"), it doesn't mean that they are comfortable and have started to take action.

Let me give you a simple analogy. Imagine Stephanie, your Millennial, is not twenty-two but a pre-teen who wants to be on the diving team at school. You are the coach of the swim team. During the try-outs, you see she is an excellent swimmer and, for a beginner, shows a lot of promise on the diving board. You welcome her to the team. The next few weeks, you explain the fundamentals of diving in detail, break down the dives in simple steps, and guide her through various diving exercises. She practices and practices, each time getting better and correcting her mistakes. One day, you decide Stephanie is ready for the real thing and announce her name to the group as a starting diver in the next competition. She seems elated and everyone congratulates her.

The day of competition arrives. The place is packed with competitors and spectators. Beaming, you go up to Stephanie and ask "You good to go?"

"I think so," she answers.

"Fantastic," you say. "You're going to do great."

Stephanie's name is announced on the loudspeaker. She climbs up the steps toward the diving board. You notice something is off right away: you've never seen her climb this tentatively—and she's looking down the whole time. It seems to take forever for her to reach the top, and the crowd starts to get restless. *It's just nerves,* you convince yourself, *it's her first time diving in a competition. She'll settle down.*

Stephanie reaches the diving board and just stands there. And stands there. She doesn't even get into the correct posture. She's frozen solid with fear. You cheer words of encouragement along with her teammates, but she doesn't budge. You ultimately realize it's not happening, and you need to get her down before it becomes traumatic for her.

Stephanie had the skills and the talent and was well prepared, but she still didn't jump off that board that day. What went wrong?

From the time you told her she was competing for real until the actual day of the event, you said *nothing of meaning to her.* A moment before the dive, you asked her if she was "good to go" and said she was going "to do great," but those are canned phrases you say to everyone. The words didn't register.

Instead, Stephanie needed constant communication and words of assurance from you throughout the week that *she was ready for this and more than prepared to compete.* She needed you to tell her over and over again that *every* great diver starts out a little afraid the first time—it's only natural. You wouldn't badger her to make her more nervous, but rather sprinkle a few words at a time to her—in person and perhaps in an encouraging e-mail—to reinforce your belief that it's "Go!" time.

Okay, let's say Stephanie is a 22-year-old sales rep. You've trained her, you've coached her, you've praised her—and you've even had her teammates collaborate with her and show her a few pointers. You have told her several times by phone and e-mail that she's *100% ready* and needs to make her first sales pitch before the end of the week. It's "Go!" time. Now she has to *go out on the field and sell.*

At a certain point, Stephanie needs to conquer her fear, take that leap, and make that all-important dive. She may do a perfect swan dive or a belly flop, but either way you are right there afterward to offer praise and support. It may take a while, but once she makes that first big sale, compliment her work and reassure her that her sales ability is so good, she should view her "Go!" switch *as always being on.*

5 Things to Remember

1. Don't assume that your Millennial reps feel that they are ready to "Go!" and sell, unless you have specifically told them so.
2. Train your team members, tell them to "Go!," coach them, praise them—and then praise them again after they have made their first pitches (whether they were successful or not).
3. Over-communicate with your direct reports in multiple ways: in person, by phone, and via e-mail.

4.   Don't micromanage by telling your team members how to do every little thing. Never do tasks for them—even if you are frustrated with their lack of action.

5.   Tell your reps that they are "100% ready" and that the "Go!" switch is always on.

·
·
·

CHAPTER FIFTEEN

GIVING THEM THE TOOLS TO OVERCOME SALES OBJECTIONS

Several years ago, I wrote *25 Toughest Sales Objections (and How to Overcome Them)*. In the book, I identify the four client personality types—Dominant, Influence, Steadiness, and Conscientious—and show how to handle objections for each one. That book holds up pretty well, so I'm not going to get into substantial detail about those types here.

The issue you are likely facing as a sales leader today is even more basic than the objection itself. You may have a team of salespeople who are not accustomed to being on the receiving end of resistance and conflict. Growing up as they did, Millennials were treated with kid gloves. If they skinned their knees riding their bikes, they were rushed to the emergency room. When I was young, there were two treatments for a skinned knee: mercurochrome (which left bigger red stains than any bleeding, and hurt like crazy) and momma's spit. After that, we hopped right back on our bikes. Somehow we all managed to survive with our beet-red knees intact.

Every sales rep has had his or her share of skinned knees (and maybe some broken bones, too) from sales meetings that went far south of the equator. Buyers come up with all kinds of reasons for resisting your pitches and declining your product or service. I don't have to tell you that sometimes they get rude, insulting, or just plain nasty. Rejection is part of the gig. As confident sales professionals, we've learned to douse the wounds with mercurochrome and get right back out on the field.

As for today's reps . . . well, they might have sales PTSD from the first turndown and struggle to recover. Why? Because you—as mommy, daddy, or both—didn't protect them from the big bad buyers and swoop in to save them when things turned ugly. Just like when they didn't realize you'd given them the "Go!" signal to start selling (see the previous chapter), they once again froze. They didn't realize they need to go back to those same buyers and try again . . . again . . . and again.

WHAT IF YOUR REP BELIEVES THE OBJECTION?

There are many young reps who interpret the phrase "the customer is always right" the *wrong way*. Millennials might even have a sense of loyalty to their buyers and defer to whatever they say as 100% fact. Your role as sales leader is to inform your reps that the customer is indeed right when it comes to a difference of opinion or complaint— *except* when it comes to a sales objection. Then you need to remind them that they work for *your company*, and it's *your company* that signs their paychecks.

Sometimes it's harder to convince your own team that an objection is false than the buyer himself. Young reps are known to overreact to resistance, especially when the answer is a flat-out "No" without further explanation. But it only takes one instance of a rep successfully asking questions, finding out the real reason behind the decline, providing solutions for the buyer, and overcoming an objection to gain enough confidence in your company's product the next time around.

First and foremost, your sales team needs to learn two things: 1) how to research as much as possible about the buyer's company, and 2) how to ask the buyer questions on what can't be found through research. Experienced sales professionals know and understand that nine times out of ten, the objection provided by the buyer is not the real or complete reason why the product was declined. It's the rep's job to expose the underlying reason *behind* that objection. Conducting extensive research and asking questions can help get to the root cause of many objections and reverse them.

Perhaps the most common sales objection is regarding price. We've all heard the phrase "Your price is too high" *ad nauseam*. Some reps automatically assume that this objection means *game over*—unless your company caves and lowers its price. Some reps see price reductions as the *only* solution. This might be the exact wrong approach to take. As soon as you start lowering prices, you are reducing the perceived value of the product, maybe even cheapening it. Your customer certainly won't want it if she thinks it's cheaply made and if you cave that easily. You are also conceding power to the buyer to dictate your company's pricing strategy, which gives them the impression that they can always tell you how to price your goods—which is *never good.*

This is where *research* comes in. Conducting research should be a snap for your Millennials. They can find pretty much any data point on their phones before you've even booted up your hard drive. So this plays to one of their strengths—and they'll probably enjoy doing it.

The rep needs to thoroughly research the client's organization. These are just a few things for her to drill into:

1. Who are their consumers/end users?
2. Is their business expanding?
3. What do they need?
4. What trends are coming up?
5. What is the buyer's pricing history?

The buyer's pricing history will help your rep determine if the buyer's objection about pricing is remotely true. Next, she needs to see how the competitors' prices stack up against those of your company. With regard to the latter, sometimes having her create a simple one-page competitive chart is enough to demonstrate that the claim "your price is too high" is unfounded. Without rubbing the buyer's nose in it, proving the buyer incorrect on this point is an easy way to get them to come around and make the purchase.

Then again, as I've said many times, everyone *always* wants a better price (or uses it as a default). Prices are negotiable, and I believe that a product only costs too much if the customer believes its value is beneath the price. The sales tactic here is to accentuate the many benefits of the product, which will more than justify the price. Research comes into play here as well, because the salesperson should be able to highlight all the value-added aspects of your product that dwarf the competition.

Now we get into the "asking questions" part. Ideally, the reps should be trained to think on their feet and ask questions during the meeting with their buyers. But if they draw a blank, can't get a word in edgewise, or just run out of time, it's perfectly fine to follow up with questions prior to a re-pitch. Usually in these cases, a friendly phone call is better than an e-mail because the rep is likely to get a quicker and more thoughtful response. There is also extra nuance that can be gleaned from a person's voice. Some buyers are poor respondents when it comes to answering e-mail, or just dislike putting things in writing.

Suppose the buyer says "I don't need the product." Your rep needs to ask whether he means his company doesn't really need the product, or he doesn't believe there is a consumer market for it. These are completely different situations, and knowing the answer can determine the follow-up strategy for the resell. If it's the latter, your rep can provide research and data to the buyer identifying the trends and the consumer market and need.

If, however, the buyer means his *company* doesn't need the product, your rep needs to find out his client's *real* problem and then work to solve it. Your salesperson must write down the answers word for word and then spend some time determining how your company and your product can best solve the client's dilemma. Within a few days of the conversation, your rep should propose solutions to the client's problem—and repeat back the exact words he heard and wrote down. In doing so, it shows that your rep was paying attention and working hard to serve his client. What buyer wouldn't want to do business with a thoughtful salesperson like that?

Millennials tend to be loyal and ethical, so, once they understand that fielding sales objections is actually supporting the client by providing solutions, they should be good to go.

5 Things to Remember

1. Recognize that Millennials may need a great deal of help fielding buyer resistance—and expect a lot of support from you.
2. Today's salespeople may believe the buyer objection at face value, so you need to work on adjusting their mindset.

3. Never allow your team to accept a first objection—especially "the price is too high"—as a final decline.
4. Your sales team must conduct substantial research and ask a lot of questions to overcome buyer objections.
5. Your reps need to find out their buyers' problems and offer your company's products and services as solutions.

CHAPTER SIXTEEN

•
•
•

KEEPING THEM FIRED UP AND AGGRESSIVE

Generally speaking, salespeople are an impatient bunch. They should be: you want them to be anxious and ravenously hungry for the next product, the next launch, and the next big sale that will line their pockets.

Sales *Millennials* are still impatient—although it may not always seem that way—especially when it comes to visualizing the path toward the next level and the future. They hear all about their friends who are making big bucks right out of college, some of whom may even have started up their own companies. Your people are always looking around at what other people are doing and at other opportunities. They may have had energy and enthusiasm for your company and products at first but, if they don't see tangible forward motion with their careers, they might bolt at the very next open position that comes their way.

When it comes to managing Millennials, you have to work extra hard to keep your team engaged and fired up to make sales. Interestingly, it's some of the softer, "squishier" things that tend to rev them up. Since they always have one eye on what their friends are doing and the other upward on the next rung on the ladder, it's worth seeing what you can do in your organization regarding creating more satisfying job titles.

Bear with me on this: in the large scheme of things, a change in job title is a small give to a strong performer so he or she feels good about working in your company and gives 110%. Don't worry, I'm not going to suggest promoting 22-year-olds to "Senior Sales Director" after one year. But you are never going to develop a well-trained, muscular, and cohesive team if your employee turnover is high. Your team is going to abandon you if they think their job titles are "small," or if they don't feel like their careers are progressing rapidly enough.

When people flip jobs with regularity, it impacts the morale of those left standing, who inherit the problems of the people who left and have to fill in their gaps. You also end up being in "constant training mode" and getting employees up to speed, which can be completely exhausting. It may take weeks before you see any benefits from new recruits. In the meantime, as each month goes by with an unfilled position, you are losing sales and don't have point people in place to give your clients the best service possible.

Above all, you need to retain people in order to build the "back bench" I discussed at length in the Introduction. Who will become your company's future sales leaders? Who will develop an in-depth understanding of the company's DNA to impart to the next generation if you can't retain the people you have?

Let's tackle this issue head-on. If "promotions" are all your team cares about, see if you can create a career ladder that takes them up *one half rung at a time.* For example, after a year, a strong performer can go from Sales Assistant to Associate Sales Rep. After two years, she can move from Associate Sales Rep to Sales Rep. After three years, perhaps there's room to become an Account Manager or Senior Rep. (I recognize that job titles and positions can vary wildly from one industry to the next, but you get the idea: baby steps up the ladder.)

WHAT'S IN A JOB TITLE?

A salesperson by any other name is . . . still a *salesperson.* True, it does sound better if you stuck "VP," "Executive," or "Director" somewhere in it, but the reality is that one title is as good as the next (as long as you are no longer using the now-verboten word "telemarketer").

However, titles matter *a lot* to Millennials. Think about the "Genius" titles given to Apple Store professionals. Who doesn't want "Genius" on his or her business card and have it validated by Apple?

With that in mind, you may want to consider "modernizing" your sales position titles—if it generates excitement among your team and helps retention efforts. Your team members might prefer "Relationship

Representative," "Client Engagement Specialist," or "Results Getter" to plain old "Sales Representative." Creativity and panache can be good things, and I'm all in favor of evolving with the times if a simple name change is all it takes.

One word of caution: don't go overboard or be overtly cute, as this could put off certain clients. You want your team to have a certain amount of pride (and fun), but a job title goes on the business card that is handed to your customers (and/or in the signature line of e-mails) and you don't want your company to be ridiculed, either. I happen to love the sound of the job title "Closer," but I wouldn't recommend using it on a business card as a title.

If job title isn't the issue, then you may need to address employee *engagement*. If the idea of pure sales doesn't incentivize your team to do cartwheels in the hallway, think about other creative ways to engage and energize them. For example, if one of your reps is into charitable causes, perhaps it's an opportunity for her to lead an effort with one of your clients to create a fundraising event. This has the dual impact of doing good for the community while at the same time getting close to your customers and enabling them to see your organization in a positive light.

Be careful, though: your involvement with the charity must seem *genuine;* if it doesn't, your team will cry "BS" and the whole effort will have been wasted. As you can see, a recurring element among Millennials is *authenticity.* They won't take too kindly to your "pretending" to believe in the cause just for the sake of good PR (or just to please them).

Sometimes it's the company structure that's bringing your team down and demotivating them. Are there too many layers of approvals? Are there too many signoffs that take forever? Are there dated processes that don't make sense, given today's technology and high-speed way of doing business?

You may *think* everything is all hunky-dory and functioning smoothly, but your team might be feeling otherwise yet can't put a finger on it. Or, they just won't tell you something is wrong with structure or process because either 1) they think you should already know, or 2) they don't think it's their place to tell you.

If you feel there is a malaise spreading through your team, you have to nip it in the bud right away and solicit specific feedback from them. Put your top team member in charge of surveying the group for improvements that can be made to unclog blockages and anything that might be a source of frustration for them. It could be as simple as a quick fix on an antiquated client database. Encourage brainstorming for the team to offer specific solutions. A tech-savvy Millennial would welcome the challenge of being empowered to fix or upgrade a flagging system held together with rubber bands and paper clips.

You'll want to be open to suggestions and allow changes wherever you can, but of course you need to make it clear from the get-go that it might not be possible to improve everything. As has been mentioned throughout this book, you also have to monitor the amount of time your sales team spends on this to make sure they aren't turning systems/process improvement into a full-time job when they should be busy selling.

If it turns out that *you* are the blockage—i.e., you take too long to respond to e-mails, get signoffs, or make decisions—then you need to wake up, develop some self-awareness, and take drastic action to improve and reverse the situation. If you get any whiff that you might be the holdup, chances are that your team is far more frustrated with you than you think—and they are looking around for another job because they believe you are the cause of their problems (whether you are or aren't). You'll want to let go of anything you can to help your team feel freed up and pumped to sell.

Sometimes salespeople lack motivation not because of their lofty career goals or frustrating processes/systems, but because they feel that they are too far removed from the company vision (see Chapter Five). In some organizations, salespeople are at the top of the food chain, whereas in others they might be more of an afterthought (i.e., "the tail of the dog" or the last part of the process chain). If it's the latter case in your company, the vision statement as written might be a complete disconnect with your team and not mean diddly-squat.

Vision statements can make a big difference to Millennials. *They want to be part of something big.* If your company's vision statement is generic and along the lines of "We strive to create the best products and services on the market that inspire people," you are going to have a hard time getting your sales team jazzed about the company and staying with it. But, if you happen to have something along the lines of Google's fabulous vision statement (*"to provide access to the world's information in one click"*), you are as good as gold!

As a sales leader, you may or may not have influence over determining the company's overall vision. (In fact, if you are part of a large corporation, you probably have zero.) But there is nothing preventing you and your team from creating your own *team* sales vision, as long as it doesn't contradict anything in the company's main vision. Your team members will feel empowered and a sense of pride and ownership.

Whatever your team's sales vision might end up being, make sure it isn't soft or squishy: it needs to *excite* and *inspire* (without specifically using either of those two overused words) and, most of all, get your team fired up to sell.

⑤ Things to Remember

1.   Watch out for early signs of employee restlessness that might mean your team is already looking around for other jobs.
2.   Millennials want rad (sorry, but I had to use the word at least once in this book!) job titles, so accommodate them if you can.
3.   One way to get Millennials engaged is to make charity part of the sales effort.
4.   Unblocking internal obstacles and repairing slow systems and processes can go a long way toward improving team enthusiasm.
5.   If all else fails to motivate your sales team, try suggesting that they create their own vision statement that gives them greater purpose and connectivity to the company.

•
•
•

RECOGNIZING THAT THEY KNOW WAY MORE ABOUT TECHNOLOGY THAN YOU

This is where the fun starts—at least for your team. Whatever you may think of technology—friend, foe, or somewhere in the middle as just another office tool—your young sales team eats, drinks, breathes, sleeps, and dreams about it. They've been immersed in it since birth and probably have more tech knowledge in their fingernails than you will ever have in your brain. They are using social media to find clients, reach clients, and pitch to clients in ways the "old guard" can't begin to fathom. But this knowledge can also cause friction between you and your reports, as well as between the "new guard" and the "old guard" among your sales team.

Here are a few helpful rules for you with coping:

1. **Don't be offended if they joke about your lack of knowledge.** Be a good sport. Let them have their laugh. You can even afford to be self-deprecating and still hold your head high. It's a generational thing, and there's nothing wrong with being a tech neophyte. You probably grew up when TV's still had rabbit ears and the only "cable" you had was the scrambled static on your UHF channels. (Remember those?)

2. **Admit they know more than you do to them.** Don't fight it. They are light years ahead of you, and it's okay to say so. They'll appreciate your honesty.

3. **Welcome their help.** If they see you are frustrated or struggling with something on your phone, laptop, or PC/Mac, they will probably offer to assist you without your even having to ask. Let them have

at it. They'll save you many IT Help Desk tickets and long waits for repair. If they don't offer help, ask for it.

4. **Don't ever pretend to know something you don't.** This is a good general rule, but it's especially true when it comes to technology and Millennials. If you try to pretend to be knowledgeable about something and fail, they will see you as a phony and won't trust you for anything thereafter.

In all likelihood, your Millennial team members are going to be the ones who volunteer to handle the videoconferencing and teleconferencing devices. They'll also be quick to master company databases and all the tools available on your company's intranet. This does *not mean they want to be IT specialists*; it simply indicates that they are adept at it and want to be useful and demonstrate to you what they can do. (And yes, sometimes they want to just show off and/or rub it in. Fine!)

So, here's the deal. They can play around with all the technology your company has to offer, as long as it 1) doesn't distract from selling efforts, 2) helps you and the team get through the day with fewer glitches and headaches, and 3) can be adapted to *improve the sales process and increase sales in some tangible fashion*. After that, you have to draw the line.

Below are some good examples of how their innate tech abilities might be able to help you, and you shouldn't hesitate to ask and/or encourage them to dig deeper into them. Imagine one of your reps has discovered the following:

- A system that tracks sales leads more efficiently than the one you are using. Take it seriously by agreeing to check out a demo and/or do a free trial run.

- A brand-new app that accelerates sales research three times faster than how you currently do it. Have your team download it and empower the rep who found it to train others on its usage.

- Documents and spreadsheets on the company intranet that may be applied to team efforts. Have the rep share them with the team.

■ An emerging social media platform that matches your customer and consumer demographic. Empower him to research the platform and create a strategy your company can exploit for sales conversion.

■ A method of video or phone conferencing that is better than what you are currently using. Give it a try, at least on a trial run.

■ A simple personalized system for managing voluminous e-mails that not only helps save company storage space, but also organizes them for simple tracking. Encourage the rep to share these techniques with the team.

■ A suggestion for adapting existing software to help streamline a process. This is a win-win, as you don't have to invest in "purchasing" new software.

■ An app that finds restaurants perfectly matching a customer's lunch preferences. This can be especially handy for finding a nearby place to eat in real time when dining with a customer who has strict dietary restrictions. (Or the customer might love a certain type of Indian dosa.) Always check with your app-savvy reps before struggling on your own to sift through hundreds of options on a Google search.

■ Any ideas that can be beneficial to a customer (buyer) or consumer (end user).

If any of the above circumstances occur, provide *positive feedback* to the rep as encouragement to come up with additional ideas along these lines. The more pats on the back you provide, the more focused the salesperson will be on finding new ways to improve your business that move the needle and serve your customers better.

By the same token, there are also instances of when technology starts to get out of hand and must be met with *corrective feedback*:

• The rep disappears for hours helping people with their computer issues.
• The rep attends non-sales-related meetings, brainstorming IT products.

- The rep spends work time on apps, on blogs, and/or on social media that have nothing to do with your products or services—and nothing to do with selling.

There are other areas of significance when it comes to technology and managing Millennial salespeople. Consider, for example, that in many cases Millennials have been raised on the art of conciseness: Tweets, brief texts, short e-mails, and emojis to represent words. Spelling may be abbreviated and/or otherwise simplified as a matter of generational habit. Their slang vocabulary is often a way to express condensed meaning, emotion, and circumstance. It's entirely possible that your Millennial reps are using this cozy, informal language in verbal and written communication to key customers, which is problematic if the individuals on the other end are from a different generation and don't "get it." If an e-mail from one of your reps is filled with Millennial "code" language, your customers might be confused and/or regard your salesperson as unsophisticated, unintelligent, careless, illiterate, or unprofessional.

I knew one sales rep who constantly referred to a customer in his seventies as *dude*. Now, I'm not saying everyone needs to be referred to as "Sir" or "Mr. Abernathy III," but *dude*? Really?

In another instance, I heard about a salesperson who was hooked on using emojis. He used a "peach" emoji in an e-mail when referring to a female customer. This e-mail was passed along in an e-mail chain until it inadvertently reached the customer herself. She was curious about what a "peach" meant, and looked it up on the Internet. Guess what—the rep was saying she has a "nice butt." She didn't take it as a compliment. This kind of stupidity not only leads to lost customers, but also potentially to terminations and lawsuits.

Is a smiley face or thumbs-up emoji going to hurt a deal? Probably not. But they can come across to some people as cheesy or unprofessional. It all comes down to knowing your customers and projecting how they might best respond to them. If *they* use emojis, then it may even be in one's best interests to respond in kind (with the appropriate ones, of course).

EMOJIS: THE MILLENNIALS' SECRET HIEROGLYPHICS

Years ago, when European Jews came to the U.S., they would speak Yiddish to each other when they didn't want their children to understand what sensitive topics they were talking about. (This probably holds true for first-generation immigrants from many places, but as a frame of reference let's stick with European Jews since it's one I know.)

When it comes to Millennials, they might be using a verbal and written language using symbols *about you* to keep you in the dark and perhaps even poke fun at you. For example, if a Millennial sends an emoji of two round eyes looking sideways, it's a tipoff of "being watched" as if to say you are acting like Big Brother. (This same graphic is also sometimes used as a flirty icon.) Any kind of food emoji—usually a fruit or vegetable—used about you (or anyone) is *not* going to be a compliment. Bananas and eggplants represent certain male anatomy, while a taco or cat face depicts—well, I'm sure you can figure those out on your own.

These are just a few examples—there are myriad more, and they continue to evolve, with new ones added every day. It's quite an education keeping up with all of it. You, as supervisor, are responsible for your team—so creating an "emoji policy" is probably a good idea.

Your team's technological knowledge and talents—combined with their ability to research and find things in milliseconds—can be channeled into positive results if handled properly. Employees who have superlative Internet searching skills, for example, should be encouraged to tap into them in order to find out as much as possible about your customers: their problems, their concerns, their challenges, their history, and their future direction. The more they know about your clients, the better they can focus their pitches and apply them appropriately. They can also avoid "sensitive areas" *not* to be mentioned or discussed with clients, such as company scandals and controversies.

The downside to all this technology is that your team members become heavily reliant on it to do pretty much everything. In certain sales situations, thinking things through on their own, gut feeling (intuition), and hands-on experience can sometimes be more valuable than a few clicks on a keyboard. We know, for example, that the Internet is filled with as much "fake news" as it is real information, and one has to be discerning to know what to trust when mining data. Figuring out which sources are reliable and trusted versus which ones are biased or just unreliable can make or break a salesperson's credibility. Imagine, for example, if your rep arms herself with data for a buyer presentation and her source is debunked midway into her speech? It's not only embarrassing, but the deal is likely sunk.

Your team of Millennials wants constant feedback, and this is the perfect place for you to provide it. They may rightly assume you know less about technology than they do, but you need to challenge the *depth* of their research, their *accuracy*, and the *validity* of the sources they use. While they are lightning-fast at finding things, they may also waste a lot of time being distracted along the way—pop-ups, links, social-media posts, etc.

When it comes to technology and research, many Millennials act like hyperactive puppies. They have intense curiosity and will randomly flit from one cool thing to the next. As you are providing feedback to them, let them know how much time they are spending "researching" vs. "selling" and provide them with a framework for self-monitoring and finding the right balance. If you can channel a Millennial's tech ability in the right way instead of ignoring or dismissing it, you will find they want to stick around longer because they are having fun, sharing it with their teammates, and contributing to the larger company effort.

5 Things to Remember

1. Let your Millennials feel pride in knowing more than you do when it comes to modern technology.
2. Never pretend you know more about technology than you really do, as your team will lose respect for you.
3. If your reps' technology skills boost your company's systems and processes, improve real-time research (and are accurate), and connect to sales efforts, encourage them to continue to apply these abilities to work.

4. If technology distracts from a rep's sales efforts, provide constructive feedback that refocuses her back on achieving sales results.

5. Emojis can be risky when it comes to usage at work (internally and with customers). Generally they should be limited to a smiley face, unless the sender is 100% certain the recipients will understand them and be receptive to them.

•
•
•

CHAPTER EIGHTEEN

SHIELDING THEM FROM
WHAT MAY CHALLENGE THEIR VALUES

Ethan, a 28-year-old sales rep for a major technology company, was about to head on a sales call to Techskill, one of his key buyers. On his way out to the airport with his suitcase, Jessica, his boss, called out to him by the elevator and said "Hey, Ethan. While you're at Techskill meeting with Ashley and Don, try to find out what you can about the new modem coming from DigiRev. Techskill does a lot of business with them, so find out anything you can—product benefits, pricing, you know. I expect a lot of intel. Now—go kill it! Thanks."

Before Ethan could say anything, the elevator door opened. Inside, the elevator was filled with restless people anxious for him to get in and the doors to close so they could go downward. He entered the elevator without having a chance to say anything to Jessica except a cursory "Bye."

While in the elevator, on the cab ride, and during the entire plane trip, Ethan fretted about trying to pull in favors from his customer about his competitor and get them to divulge company secrets to him. He wasn't sure what to make of this; it just felt *wrong*. *How can I work for a company with such bad ethics?* he wondered.

When it comes to fair play, Millennials tend to have a strong sense of ethics and frown upon others who don't meet their standards. They are going to recoil at having to perform an unethical act—even if it falls into a "gray area." In the above scenario, Ethan might have done one of the following things: followed orders and obtained the information against his better judgment; or made a conscious decision *not* to obey his boss's request. In both situations, the Millennial is disgusted by his boss, Jessica—but won't tell her. He feels icky about working for her and for a company that would have the audacity to ask him to do such a thing. In all likelihood, Ethan started looking for another job as soon as he returned home from his business trip.

Short of anything illegal, old-school sales reps would do whatever it took to make a sale. In some cases, being able to walk that fine tightrope just right and get what they wanted, no matter what, was part of the excitement and story to tell after the trip. Millennials, however, don't like "cheating" at all. In fact, they might feel that their competitors deserve equal knowledge about *your* company, since that would be fair play.

When offering instruction and advice to Millennials in "gray ethics areas," be responsible and attuned to how they might interpret what you are suggesting they do. Your guidance may be perfectly legal and within the guidelines of your company's code of ethics, but your young salespeople still might not get it. You need to take the time to explain what you have in mind, why it's important, and why it isn't any kind of "ethics" issue. If you find that you are struggling to defend any of these points, then either: (1) question why you are doing it and perhaps change your mind; or (2) find someone else (preferably of parallel rank to yourself) to shield your high ethics rep and do your dirty work for you. It's not worth setting off a chain of events you'll regret, such as your sales rep speaking with HR or upper management about you.

PRACTICE WHAT YOU PREACH

If you want your team to be loyal to you and to your company, you need to demonstrate a high level of ethical behavior at all times. "Walking the walk and talking the talk" means the obvious major things (such as not taking advantage of a client or customer), as well as the day-to-day things (such as following your company's paper-recycling guidelines).

Don't take anything for granted. For example, as a sales leader, you should never mistreat any of your vendors, clients, or partners—even if you feel they deserve retaliation for something they might have done to you. On a smaller scale, you never want to be heard by a team member badmouthing a vendor, client, or customer—even if it's with another company executive. It's obvious advice, but I'll offer it anyway:

keep yourself clean and out of any HR trouble (especially any office romances!). You need to serve as a role model for your team. They look for you to take the high road, which in business means you should always have your hiking boots on.

Someone once said to me: "If you wouldn't want to see something as a headline in the *New York Times*, then don't write it, say it, do it, or click send."

Along these lines, any kind of phoniness and lying will also be negatively regarded by Millennials. If, for example, you tell a client that you love golf in front of a Millennial the day after you admitted how much you hate it, that Millennial won't see you as acting clever to win over a client; she'll see you as a fraud. And, if you ask the Millennial to pretend that she loves golf to a client when she's never lifted a club, you can be sure she'll be downstairs talking to upper management and HR about your having asked her to do something unethical. It may sound overboard on something as trivial as golf, but these things happen and are not worth the risk.

Millennial ethics materialize in other ways that are mentioned elsewhere in this book. They crave working for a company that has *a purpose, a mission,* and a *vision.* If working at your company is just about a paycheck, then the "ethics" piece comes to the fore because they don't want to work someplace that's solely concerned with pure greed. These are some other things they might be looking for in their places of employment:

- Products or services that help individuals or society.
- Companies that offer environment-friendly products or services.
- Companies that give back to charity in some fashion.
- Companies that treat employees equally, fairly, and with respect.
- Companies that are "authentic" with their products and services and deliver on what they promise.

If you can encourage any of the above in your company, your reps will be even more motivated to perform. They will be pumped and have pride in working for your company—even if the salary, commissions, and bonuses aren't top dollar.

On the other hand, if a Millennial employee witnesses anything they consider to be unethical behavior or feels your company treats others with "disrespect," they will resign in a heartbeat without feeling a shred of regret. They are also extremely dedicated to their co-workers and teams, so if they see people are being wrongly treated in their organization, they will also head right to the career websites to seek other opportunities. The moral judgments don't stop there: if they observe that someone on your team has behaved unethically but don't see that you are actively doing something about it (even if you have done so behind the scenes), they will hold you responsible.

By the way, I'm not suggesting that this generation is more "ethical" than past generations, but rather that they are more sensitive with regard to certain things. Ironically, there are areas of ethics that Millennials stomp all over, such as content downloading. The younger generation is used to getting everything for free online—songs, videos, books, articles, pix, apps, you name it—and they think the Internet is a copyright- and trademark-free playground where they can just "get stuff."

The whole mindset of sharing music, books, videos, and the like is nice for those doing it—but, of course, it has caused a lot of creative work to be devalued and for artists to lose out on a great deal of royalty money. But many Millennials don't see the ethical dilemma in this, because it's how they were raised and "everybody is doing it."

In the office, you probably need to keep your eyes open for team members who randomly download stuff (apps, videos, articles, etc.) that may encroach on ethical and/or legal issues. These acts may seem innocent, but you don't want any of that to come back to bite your employee—or your department or company.

Earlier in this book, I mentioned that Millennials need freedom and creative space. They can't feel restricted about their jobs or be chained to a desk from 9:00 to 5:00. If you've granted them the freedom and privilege of flex hours—which requires a great deal of trust on your part—you don't want to hear that an employee who called in with a hurt leg has been spotted at the gym running on a treadmill. Or that a sales rep who called in sick with the flu was seen at the beach by a fellow manager who had a real vacation day. Ethics and trust are two-way streets.

Sometimes the ethical dilemmas do not involve you, your company, or your rep. Instead, they concern your *customers*. If a vendor, partner, or customer—including one of great stature—is doing something overtly illegal and/or unethical, it stands to reason that you'll find a way to stop doing business with that entity. On the other hand, if an essential vendor, partner, or customer does something that falls into the "gray area" and you have no choice except to continue with business as usual, what do you do then?

Obviously, you only want to work with the best, most ethical people possible. But there is no real way for anyone to know every aspect of how companies do business. We are always shocked when we read headlines about an individual or company's bad behavior that leads to indictments and such. It's not up to you to judge, but you are entitled to back out of relationships that might damage and drag down your company's reputation. If you decide to look the other way or truly don't know what the other side is up to, then proceed at your own risk.

If you do press forward, aligning with a sketchy customer, you have to explain things to your Millennial team members who may judge your company based on the people with whom you are doing business. Be transparent with your team, but also agree to pull out at the first sign of trouble. If someone remains uncomfortable, it's fine for you to reassign the account to someone who doesn't have an issue with the customer.

Lastly—and perhaps most importantly—always have your team's back. If someone inside or outside your organization behaves unethically to your team member, you need to jump in and hold that person accountable.

In one instance, I knew of one buyer who insulted a young sales rep and brought her to tears. I told her manager that he needed to step up and call the buyer to let him know this didn't sit well. The manager did just that. He diplomatically summarized what had happened and claimed his rep felt insulted and disrespected. The buyer, who said he didn't realize what he was doing (whether this is true or not is up for debate), called the rep right after and profusely apologized. While on the line with her, he doubled his order for the product.

No doubt this positive result was out of guilt, but who cares? The message was made loud and clear by the sales leader: *I have my team's back. If you mess with them, you mess with me!*

5 **Things to Remember**

. . . .

1. Never ask a Millennial team member to do anything that might go up against his or her code of ethics—even if there is nothing illegal about it and it doesn't infringe upon the company's policies and practices.
2. Always set a good ethics example for your team.
3. Some Millennials regard everything on the Internet as "free"; be 100% certain that they are aware of and respect copyright and trademark ownership at all times.
4. If you must do business with a "sketchy" customer, don't force the account on a Millennial rep who might be offended; rather, hand it off to someone who is comfortable with the relationship.
5. Always have your team's back!

•
•
•

CHAPTER NINETEEN

HELPING THEM MAKE A GOOD IMPRESSION

Be honest. If a salesperson has a nose ring, a tongue ring, and or tattoos snaking all over their neck, throat, and arms, would you hire that person? If you were a buyer for a large corporation and a sales rep came into your office wearing torn jeans and a T-shirt, would you trust him enough to make a substantial purchase from this individual?

I'm not judging anyone who has tattoos or piercings. I couldn't care less. In fact, there are probably some types of businesses—such as in the entertainment industry—where being adorned like a Christmas tree provides street cred and can actually help *make* a sale.

But if you happen to be in an industry that remains old-fashioned and conservative in its style and business approach, you would probably think twice before hiring someone who does not present up to a certain visual standard. Here's the thing: according to the Pew Research Center, over 40% of Millennials have at least one tattoo. By the same token, 63% of adults over the age of sixty *disapprove* of tattoos. That leaves a lot of potential buyer declines occurring simply because the customer doesn't like the look of the salesperson. Some might even be *afraid* of a person with a nose ring or tattoo.

There are many people (not just business professionals) who would rightfully be offended by a tattoo of a swastika, nude figure, or anything depicting blood or violence. Clearly, you can't have a salesperson parading around representing your company while having any of these types of things showing on his or her skin.

But what about the gray areas, like a tattoo of the hard rock band Megadeth or even a sultry depiction of a costumed superhero like Wonder Woman? Where does one draw the line?

Of course, the buyer won't specifically tell the rep whether he or she is offended by or dislikes the salesperson's appearance. The relationship will simply come to a screeching halt and the orders will stop. Sometimes, however, if you know the buyer and see that orders have suddenly ceased, you can do a friendly "check-in" with her and try to find out how and why this happened. Some buyers won't want to get anyone in trouble with negative feedback (or seem biased) and provide a BS response ("Oh, we're just on a tight budget for now"), but others will give you an honest (if indirect) answer to the question: "What did you think of Connor, my rep?" The oblique answer says it all: "Oh, you know . . . Connor is, well, *Connor*. He's a very interesting guy, if you know what I mean."

There are internal sand traps of poor employee presentation as well. Suppose the CEO of your company decides to spontaneously meet with your sales team for one reason or another. As soon as she sits down, she sees your female sales professional with a shiny pink hoop nose ring or your male sales professional with a monstrous skull tattoo sprouting between the top buttons of his shirt. The CEO looks as if she: (a) has lost faith in your ability to hire professional people; (b) is about to call the cops; or (c) faint from shock.

Some job candidates wisely follow advice from friends, family, mentors, and career consultants and remove the visible piercings and cover up their tattoos when heading out for job interviews. You may even have unknowingly hired someone who usually enjoys presenting himself this way and only found out later when the employee's tattoos are revealed and the piercings are on full display. It's also possible that the salesperson had the piercings done later, while employed in your company, and strolled into the office one day looking like a pincushion. Surprise!

As a hiring manager and sales leader, you'll need to put your personal tastes and opinions aside and make some difficult decisions. These are some important questions you need to ask yourself:

- What is the appropriate code of appearance for your industry (if there is one)?
- What is the culture of your organization?
- What might your customers think of a tattooed rep?
- What might your customers think of a pierced rep?

- How can you let your team enjoy freedom, confidence, and independence if you establish restrictions?
- Does the tattooed/pierced rep have genuine sales potential?

I've known several talented salespeople over the years who have had tattoos and/or piercings. They have been smart enough to cover up as needed whenever the situations arose. Nobody has ever dug in and said "This is who I am. If the customer doesn't like it, she can take it or leave it."

The fact is, a good salesperson cares about the company and about *making sales*. Whether man or woman, a dedicated sales professional should not be offended by being told he or she needs to cover up or remove a piece of jewelry. Most will see the wisdom in doing so, especially if it impacts the company's reputation, their careers, and their bank accounts.

Here's the deal. As previously mentioned, 40% of Millennials have tattoos and piercings—many of whom will ultimately find a way to move up the ladder. This means that, at some point in the future, we may start seeing senior executives who could be mistaken for attendees at a 1970s Sex Pistols concert. Cool—sort of.

Until the above happens, though, we all have to respect one person above all: *the customer*. This means you and your rep must consider everyone who works at your customer's business—from the receptionist to the head buyer to the CEO to anyone in between who your salesperson might potentially encounter. If you have any suspicion that the customer might not take to your sales rep's appearance, you have to diplomatically take action to make sure that he or she is presentable—even if it means risking offending your employee. Your customer and your company's reputation come first. In fact, even if you *don't know* the customer for a first meeting with a buyer, I wouldn't take the slightest chance. The rep needs to take off the nose ring and tongue ring and hide any tattoos. Why risk putting off a customer before your company even had the chance to make the pitch?

It's possible that your company already has a dress code that covers things like piercings and tattoos. If so, make sure to enforce it. If your company doesn't have one, work with the HR department to create one. If it's old, update it to the present-day norms.

You are probably wondering: *What if I can't find enough suitable candidates to fill up my back bench with these criteria? Some Millennials may not want to work in a place where they can't be themselves. It's hard enough recruiting good people.*

Here's the reality: If they aren't willing to respect your company policies and your customers, you don't need or want them on your team. If they were clever enough to keep off the nose ring and hide the tattoos during the interviews, they should be smart enough to know they have to do the same for certain business situations. They can make their statements of individualism when they aren't on work time representing the company.

It does seem astonishing to me that some Millennials don't know how to dress appropriately for work. Internet startups and TV show depictions of businesses today have certainly created impressions of a more casual work environment, which is true up to a point. But I want to pull my hair out when I see male sales reps who dress in torn jeans and a T-shirt that says "Just Chillaxin" or a female sales rep who dresses too provocatively. (I won't go into greater detail about the latter—you get it.)

It's ironic that some Millennials who demand respect from the company don't reciprocate by dressing appropriately for the work culture. How hard is it to buy a blazer, a buttoned-down shirt, slacks, and nice shoes? The funny thing is that they *genuinely may not know how to dress for work*; mommy and daddy may not have told them.

YOUR TEAM SHOULD DRESS LIKE EVERY DAY IS AN INTERVIEW

I tend to be old-school when it comes to proper dress for salespeople.

For a man, think Howard Schultz, Starbucks CEO: designer suit, tie, good shoes, well groomed, manicured fingernails.

For a woman, think Facebook COO Sheryl Sandberg: smart business suit, snazzy shoes, designer handbag/briefcase, some tasteful jewelry, painted fingernails (no glitter or mixed colors), salon-approved hair, and some makeup (not overdone).

Do all businesses need their salespeople to wear ties? Certainly not.

Do all women need to dress like fashion models? No way (unless you happen to be in the fashion industry, of course).

Whether your company is business casual (without so much as a sports jacket) or just plain casual (jeans), it's always smart to encourage your team to *look good* and *professional* around the office—as well as outside the office. You never know when a VIP will show up—a senior executive, a board member, the CEO of one of your biggest accounts, etc.—and you want your team to serve as a positive reflection of your company and you.

This means: lead by example. If you dress appropriately at all times, there is a good chance that they will too.

In any case, here are some good rules of thumb for any organization—even the most casual culture (except for some .com startups, perhaps): no torn jeans (not even the stylish kind), no sneakers (yes, I know Steve Jobs presented in them—but *he was Steve Jobs*), no T-shirts (especially with logos of any kind), and no shorts (unless you work in Bermuda, of course). For women, nothing too revealing—okay?

The world has become pretty lax when it comes to work clothes, which means that, if your team spiffs themselves up a notch better than the competition, it will only help set a good overall impression. A buyer is only going to praise a rep for "looking good," not for dressing down to "look chill."

If your Millennial team balks in any way at "dressing right for work," remind them of how much they like to have pride in the company they work for when it comes to other things. Dressing right might help them connect with the concept of *respect* and work toward honoring it.

If you do need to have this discussion with a sales rep—whether male or female—tread lightly. You want to explain the company dress code—whatever it might be—and why it's important from both the company and customer's perspectives. Emphasizing that it's about *respect* and *company pride* will have far more resonance to them than saying these are "the rules" or it's "company policy." (Also note: if you say "I didn't make the policy," this implies that you don't support it—which is problematic, as the employee won't buy into it either.)

Try to give your team as much creative freedom to express themselves on casual Fridays, half days, or weeks when things settle down and it's unlikely they will have a buyer encounter (such as during a holiday week). Allow them to see you loosen up and dress down after work for drinks or at an event (such as a comedy show).

Whatever you do, do not preach to them! If you lecture them, Millennials will once again see you as the Charlie Brown parents (*"wah-wah-wah"*) and tune you out. Also don't pretend to be "cooler" than you really are ("Oh, I once had a piercing on my. . . .") as it won't ring true and will fall flat. Simply appeal to their sense of teamwork, loyalty, long-term ambition, and commitment to the organization and they will probably fall in line.

5 Things to Remember

1. Visible tattoos and piercings should be avoided by your sales team if you want them to look professional and not risk losing sales for a reason within their control.

2. Customers do notice the presentation of your reps and may have hidden biases against certain types of clothing and adornment; professionalism is always the best bet.

3. If your company does not have a dress code, work with your HR department to create one; if it does, enforce it.

4. When it comes to professional appearance, lead by example.

5. In order to get "buy-in" from Millennials with regard to professional appearance, appeal to their sense of loyalty.

CHAPTER TWENTY

CREATING A FUN, INTERACTIVE, AND MEANINGFUL WORK ENVIRONMENT

No matter how cool or "chill" you think you are, the Millennials on your team will always see you as something of a relic—whether they admit it to you or not. (If you haven't heard anything specific, count on it being the latter.) You probably take your job and your work quite seriously, which is how it should be. The problem, unfortunately, is exactly that: your team doesn't think of work as *work*, they see it as *play*. To the younger generation, *work* and *play* are interchangeable. They are looking to serve in a workplace that is engaging and, most of all, *fun*.

This is where the older generations tend to get confused and lost. "What do you mean I'm 'not fun'?" you protest. "I tell jokes all the time! I brought in bagels and donuts for our meeting the other day! I binge-watch *Stranger Things*, just like they do!"

You might consider yourself the life of the party among your peers, but Millennials are probably thinking you're lame and are chuckling at you behind your back. That's fine. Generational gaps are normal and how things should be—up to a point.

If you are too out of touch with your team's needs, you'll lose their focus and probably their interest in working for you and staying with your company. Although they see you as a dinosaur, they have preconceived notions of you as the "adult" (aka mommy, daddy, etc.) and the "authority." They expect you to provide an enjoyable environment for them, explain everything to them, handhold them, and provide fun, meaning, and *purpose* for them in their jobs.

To them, *having fun* doesn't (necessarily) mean goofing around and being unproductive. But it does require you to work harder to keep their enthusiasm at a high level at all times. If they are bored, they will get lazy and/or unfocused and probably leave for the more "exciting" next opportunity.

In Chapter Five, I suggested things like setting up a video-game console or ping-pong table in the office. If you have the space indoors or outdoors, you may also be able to set up a basketball hoop. Note: If you do invest in one or more of these things, encourage your team to play them! Hold friendly competitions every now and then, too.

Or you can come up with your own creative method of helping your team release some aggression and friendly competitiveness. Frisbee football requires only a cheap piece of plastic and some running space. I know of one sales team that held indoor bocce competitions. (Sounds weird, I know, but it actually fired everyone up, despite marks left on the walls from the bocce balls.)

Developing that fun and competitive environment may not even have to involve physical competition. You could simply have regular video-game competitions. Find out what *they* like to play and try to accommodate it. (Guitar Hero can be a lot of fun, but these things do go in and out of vogue.)

It's important that you never do anything to discourage people from playing the games once you set them in motion. Let them decide on their own if they have the time or bandwidth to participate. An innocent remark or facial expression from you can deflate all the fun pretty quickly. You may also wish to alert other department heads in advance about your intentions, so they don't splash cold water on the activities. Perhaps employees from other departments can even join in and compete at some point.

Depending on your company culture and what your HR department will allow, there are other things you can do to lighten the mood. One executive I know used to bring out Nerf rifles every Friday afternoon and let her people shoot it out. For that organization, it was a goofy and successful way to let off steam—especially on occasions when the executive ended up being the first victim.

GETTING TO *REALLY KNOW* YOUR TEAM
THROUGH ASSESSMENTS

With cooperation from your HR director—and probably her participation to arrange and manage the proceedings as proper training—you may want to investigate reputable behavioral surveys, such as Myers-Briggs, StrengthsFinder, or Enneagram with your team and yourself. All examine work behaviors and strengths/weaknesses in some scientific way (no, it's not astrology!), but through different lenses. The goal is not to judge people—there is no right or wrong—but to have a greater understanding of what drives each individual's workplace behaviors. If handled correctly, team members will have a blast taking the online surveys and then sharing their results with each other. Within an hour, you'll hear them say things like "Oh, my god, it describes me exactly!," "I'm an ENTP—what are you?," or "My strengths are *Strategy, Restorative,* and *Woo!*"

I'll simplify a real story of how Myers-Briggs worked to help a relationship between a sales leader (Heidi) and sales rep (Ashley). For now, let's focus on the last letter of the two profiles: J (Judgment) and P (Perceiving). Heidi had a *J* which, despite the sound of it, means "needing to have things decided" (or "closure"). Ashley, a *P*, was the exact opposite, meaning she "likes to stay open and respond to whatever happens" (or "continuous improvement"). In the latter case, Heidi was enforcing closure on Ashley when she wasn't ready and still welcoming inputs and feedback, which caused conflict on both sides. By understanding the differences in their work styles, they were able to meet in the middle and gain the benefit of both *constant improvement* and *closure.*

Interestingly, the *Perceiving* preference is also about "mixing work and play." Sound familiar?

What else counts as both work and fun for Millennials? *Technology,* of course. If you remember any of the following things, you are leagues behind them in the technology department:

1. Typewriters in the office.
2. Your first desktop computer.

3. Your first laptop computer.
4. Your first dot-matrix printer.
5. Your first SENT e-mail.
6. You went online and heard a ton of buzzing noises.
7. You did all your sales reports and purchase orders by hand.
8. You made cold calls from a phone booth.

When new technology was added in your workplace years ago, you probably had some fear and frustration. You bought *Dummies* computer books. You made mistakes. Software didn't always cooperate. You had to undergo training with each step of Word, Excel, PowerPoint, etc. Eventually, you learned to let go of your old ways of doing things and accept technology as a useful tool and an occasional friend. But every now and then you may still get stuck because you've forgotten your fifteenth computer password or are struggling to figure out how to do something in an Excel spreadsheet.

Millennials, of course, never needed basic computer-skills training and never needed to buy a computer book. They aren't losing track of their passwords. They "got it" (technology, that is) as soon as they were two years old, grabbed your mobile phone, and figured out how to speed-dial grandma. There was never any "stress" when it came to technology.

What did they see, feel, and experience? Fun, engagement, problem-olving, lightning-fast answers, and immediate connectivity with people. By the time Millennials entered the workplace, the major technological bugs were long ironed out (except for security, but that's a whole other thing).

What this means to you is that every team meeting, every 1:1 meeting, and every assignment needs to be interactive in some fashion. To Millennials, *interactivity* is another sense, in addition to sight, smell, hearing, feeling, and taste. Interactivity to Millennials means *engaging with people and with technology at the same time.*

If you are working to solve a sales challenge or objection, for example, involve the entire team (with an agenda and time limit, of course) and keep them busy during the meeting by delegating responsibility. Don't ever just let them sit there listening to you babble on.

Here are some ways to stimulate an entire team all at once:

- One team member (other than you) leads the meeting.
- One team member writes on the whiteboard.
- One team member is on a laptop doing online research.
- One team member is managing a screen to demo videos, websites, products, etc.
- One team member creates and organizes a folder on the team's shared drive on the network.
- One team member handles the teleconferencing or video-conferencing system.
- One team member takes notes on a Word doc to add to the shared folder.

Not every task in the above list is "essential"; you could easily add to or subtract from it. But you get the idea. If you give your sales-people specific roles and involve technology, they will pay attention during the meeting. If you have a "no cell phone" rule, they won't be upset, because they are still being engaged. But even if someone does "cheat" for one minute, let it go. Have faith that the text or e-mail was important, and also know that they are more than capable of multi-tasking. (If it gets out of hand, though, you should mention it to the employee later.)

Brainstorming and problem-solving as a team using technology will be a tremendous benefit in filling the employees' need for work and play at the same time. Along with having a mission and a vision, it will also help your team find unity and cohesion.

However, these things may still not be enough to get individuals to stay in your company for the *long run*. There is one critical thing missing that holds everything together. What are they looking for? Meaning and *purpose*.

I know what you're thinking: *This is ridiculous. How many of these squishy things do I need to be doing? Am I going to spend all my time playing games, creating a mission, vision—and now a purpose?*

If you want employee retention, the answer is *Yes*: *It's essential to create a purpose*. When you were young and fired up in sales, you may not have cared about this at all: You wanted to break sales records, and that was plenty. Past salespeople who worked for you may even have been skeptical about *purpose, mission,* and *vision* and ignored them as stupid to focus on selling.

Mark my words: Today's salespeople become snarky and disinterested if you *don't* have these things.

Providing *purpose* is not as hard as it seems. It's not about faith in the religious sense, which can be a dangerous path to tread on (unless your business or organization happens to concern spirituality). Generally, they are looking for a *purpose* that *gives back* in some way to individuals and/or the community.

Many companies struggle with this notion. You probably aren't a non-profit. What if the product or service doesn't seem to have the resonance of "giving"? What if your company researches marketing data? What if your company runs a food service? What if your company distributes toilet tissue? (How much *purpose* can there be in that?)

In all these instances and many others, you can help your sales team find *purpose,* which will enable them to better connect with your product or service. The main message is that your company stands for something and *helps people in some direct or even indirect way.* If your team finds this, it will energize them to sell more.

In the above business examples, here are some ways of framing *purpose:*

1. Research marketing data: *We help our customers connect with their customers.*
2. Food service: *We help provide healthy nutritional options for schoolchildren.*
3. Toilet tissue: *We provide extra comfort for people.*

Determine what you can do to find meaning and *purpose* for your team by translating and boiling down the benefits your company offers to its customers. The object is to try to appeal to your employees on an *emotional* level. Once you do, you must personally exemplify that *purpose.* If you just throw some nice words at them and don't live and breathe it, all of your good-faith efforts will fail. For example, if your business is manufacturing and distributing toilet tissue, then don't make jokes about it that detract from the *purpose.* Even if you think you are lightening things up and providing fun, your team will think you are making fun of the product and you are diminishing its *purpose of helping provide comfort for people.* You also need to stop the senior salespeople on your team from cracking jokes about the product, as even this type of culture will put off some people. It goes without saying that if this does occur, resist laughing, no matter how funny it might be, because your team will think you are disrespecting the product as well.

Unlike Mission and Vision, however, you probably don't want to create a team brainstorming meeting about *purpose.* For starters, they expect *you* to provide this for *them.* They also won't tell you that they are searching for a *purpose* (at least in those exact words) until they are out interviewing with other companies. They only know that "something is missing" and feel you should already know how to provide it, even though they can't express what it is. Secondly, *purpose* can be such a soft, intangible thing for salespeople to discuss that I think they would spend hours on it coming up with something you'll probably feel is either cliché or too lofty.

Instead, provide opportunities on a personal level during 1:1 meetings to gauge their insights on how *they feel* about your company and what their product represents to them. Find out their areas of interest and hobbies. In all likelihood, they will not only tell you about their passions and long-term ambitions (which might be your job or CEO), they will also share some personal things about themselves and their families.

This is where your homework and creative thinking comes in. Your objective is to find something in their lives—their passions, long-term goals, or family situations—and connect it to your company's offerings. If you can successfully achieve this, your Millennial will be able to find personal meaning to what he or she is doing, feel good about it, and translate that to the outside world.

All right, so back to the toilet tissue example. (You didn't think I would let it go *that* easily now, did you?) If *providing extra comfort for people* doesn't offer enough meaning, then maybe you heard just a little something from your rep during your 1:1 that can help. It could just be one statement you hear that does the trick: "My grandfather, who has colon cancer, now lives at home with my parents. He insists on using our company's toilet tissue. My parents buy only our brand because it's comfortable for him and makes him happy."

There you go: that story is the sales pitch right there. When meeting with the buyer, your rep can tap into his grandfather's situation and explain the value proposition to anyone. Your rep is fully convinced that the product delivers on its promise and can convey its benefits to the buyer on an emotional level. I guarantee that the buyer will remember the grandfather's story and will always ask your rep how his grandfather is doing.

With all this in mind, why would the rep want to look for another job when he is selling a product that provides comfort to his grandfather *and* helps him develop a deep relationship with his buyer? The rep is far less likely to leave this source of pride behind to fly off someplace else.

This is how you create and retain your back bench of sales stars.

5) Things to Remember

1. Millennials perceive work and play as interchangeable.
2. Try to encourage your team to take an hour out of every week to play friendly competitive sports or video games with each other.
3. Bring technology into meetings as much as possible.
4. In meetings, assign roles to everyone to help team members feel active and engaged.
5. Help connect your team members to your company and product or service by creating a *purpose*.

.
.
.

CHAPTER TWENTY-ONE

COAXING THEM TO DO STUFF THEY DON'T WANT TO DO

This is probably the #1 "*Duh*" statement I could possibly make: *Making sales is the #1 priority for all salespeople.* But honestly ask yourself these two questions:

1. Is your team really cruising 180 mph on *sales* at all times?
2. Are they breathing, thinking, eating, drinking, and sleeping *sales* every hour of the day?

Somehow, I doubt the answer is "Yes" to either of the above. So what might be holding them back? I'll provide the child's answer: "*I don't wanna*."

There is stuff that needs to get done at work that no red-blooded salesperson likes to do: paperwork, data entry, spreadsheets, and so forth. Then there are the tasks that *Millennial* salespeople don't like to do and procrastinate on or entirely avoid for various reasons. If these latter items fall under prospecting, cold-contacting, pre-selling, pitching, reselling, and other core sales functions, then you have a major problem. You need to find out *why*—and *pronto*.

There are many reasons why your team might be struggling. *Boredom* is one. If that's the reason and you've truly done everything possible to engage them as mentioned in prior chapters, then you need to find new salespeople who have some raging fire in the belly to break sales records.

Here are a few possible other reasons why they don't want to do something—all of which are controllable:

1. Systems are getting in their way.
2. The process is too structured for them.
3. The work environment feels too bureaucratic or hierarchical for them.
4. They feel micromanaged.
5. They feel stuck because they aren't getting enough feedback. (Yes, we're back to this old trope.)

To tackle the above, I suggest you try the "*What If...*" exercise. In each of the examples below, try to think of the worst-case scenario of what might happen if you were to react in a certain extreme way to prod a stuck rep into doing a task he or she doesn't like or want to do.

1. Systems are getting in their way.

   What if you were to allow your reps to work around a cumbersome system?

2. The process is too structured for them.

   What if you were to forego a process that drains their creative energy?

3. The work environment feels too bureaucratic or hierarchical for them.

   What if you were to ditch all traces of bureaucracy and hierarchy that didn't break company policy or disrespect anyone?

4. They feel micromanaged.

   What if you were to back off telling your team HOW to do things?

5. They feel stuck because they aren't getting enough feedback.

   What if you were to double the amount of constructive feedback you provide every week?

If the positive outcomes of the above can lead to your salespeople generating sales yet do not lead your company into a worst-case scenario—i.e., a state of chaos and ruin—then *do it.* Give it a try on a trial basis (thirty or sixty days) and see how it goes. The more freedom and empowerment you grant, the less constrained they will feel about the activity.

With regard to #1 and #2: Are you able to delegate the systems work and process management to sales administrators and assistants? If you don't have supportive people on your team, can you budget for them?

Yes, there is head count and cost to consider in the above—but clerical/admin/systems work is drudgery for most salespeople. For many Millennials, they would prefer to eat their own hair rather than do these tasks that are bogging them down and draining their sales energy. If you have a sales support team in place—people who don't mind performing these tasks, are good at them, and see them as learning opportunities and stepping-stones—your reps will have no excuse for being unable to focus on the big picture.

With regard to #3: You may be able to take ownership and pave the way for helping alleviate company bureaucracy and hierarchy. You would need to identify the real pain points for your team, and partner with HR and/or the executive team. If your company is locked in as old-school and conservative, then your job is to do your best to shield your team from the formalities that make them uncomfortable.

With regard to #4: Micromanaging can be an especially difficult challenge for you to tackle. You may not recognize if and when you are doing it and, quite possibly, have little or no control over your own personality and behaviors (which is *not* an excuse, mind you). The conundrum is that you need your team to produce—and you know from your own experience what will work and what won't. You can see right away when they are headed down the wrong path and have an irresistible urge to *prevent it* or *fix it.* But if you keep telling a Millennial *how* to do something or are always second-guessing her, she will feel micromanaged and recoil at the task. She will lose confidence entirely and dread trying it on her own in the future. If her way of doing something won't ruin the company, let her have at it. Give her the chance to succeed or fail, take ownership of the outcome, and learn from it. Who knows? Maybe she will find an even better way of doing something and prove you wrong. Again, go back to *what if:* What is the worst thing that could happen if you were to let go of the reins? Mistakes might abound—but so might *sales!*

With regard to #5: The paradox is that your Millennial may be stuck on both #4 and #5 (feedback) at the same time. Brittany may hate being micromanaged by you and it's holding her back, but she simultaneously needs your constant feedback and reassurance.

The point of the matter is that Brittany does not want you to assign something and tell her exactly *how* to do it. She wants to ride with her intuition, creativity, and gut feeling and play around with it in her own way. Great. Let Brittany *do it.* But each week during your 1:1, you need to ask how it's progressing and what challenges she's facing. Then you need to offer specific constructive feedback on her performance and things she could try next time. You don't need to hold back. Tell it like it is: "You need to dig deeper to find out what the customer really wants." Once again, you are not telling her exactly *how* to conduct research next time, but rather, you are providing constructive insights into how you think she performed on her own. She will probably take your feedback seriously and try her best to implement it—as long as you follow up next time to reassert the same feedback. (Reminders and repetition are always good!)

NEVER CRITICIZE IN PUBLIC

Your team members need constant feedback—and you need to be honest with them about their performance. Providing feedback in the right way can make or break a salesperson. If you are too soft and shirk the main issue, your rep won't get the message. If you are too harsh, your rep will feel devalued and demotivated. It's always good practice to highlight the "good" before the "bad," and then wrap up with the "good" and an action plan.

The one thing you should *never ever* do: criticize a rep in front of others. It doesn't matter who is in the room: peers, upper management, or (especially) clients. You may think it's a "real-time lesson" and thickens their skin, but it is considered embarrassing, degrading, and unprofessional by Millennials. (Old-school sales reps may have had thicker skins and didn't mind an occasional laugh at their own expense.) If you do this in front of others, these witnesses will have a poor impression of your employee that will linger—even if it's just a solitary instance or the employee learns from the moment and never makes the mistake again. Most of all, though, your Millennial—and possibly others—will think you are a bully and don't have the backs of your team members.

When your rep says or does something inappropriate, do try to stop it at that moment. But then take it offline and discuss it at length in private at the earliest possible opportunity.

Of course, feedback goes both ways. Try to solicit feedback from your reps about yourself. Specifically ask them if you are providing enough helpful feedback—or if it's tipping over to micromanaging. Ask them what works for them and what doesn't. The transparency will go a long way toward earning and retaining their trust.

Lastly, your Millennial might not be doing something simply because mommy and daddy didn't put an award certificate on the refrigerator to provide positive reinforcement. Sometimes a Millennial can have all the tools, talent, smarts, and aggressiveness, but is lacking that extra applause from you to let her know she's on the right track. If she doesn't get recognition in some fashion, she'll lose confidence or enthusiasm—or just feel neglected.

Even if your team members seem to be on the right path, provide positive feedback, praise them, do public "shout-outs," and personally thank them. Even a small reward (such as a $10 Starbucks card) can go a long way toward showing appreciation. If you think they are again seeing you as a Charlie Brown adult ("*wah-wah-wah*") because you are doling out *too much praise* and it's coming across as stale or empty, loop in the president or CEO and have him or her offer the compliment (or gift) directly to the employee.

Positive reinforcement goes a long way. The next time your team members don't want to do something important, they'll remember your feedback, your praise, and the reward, and will feel incentivized enough to press forward with the task.

5 **Five Things to Remember**

1. To help your sales team focus on the important tasks they don't want to do (i.e., selling!), start out by finding out *why* they don't want to do it.

2. Try the *What if* exercise to determine the worst-case scenario by allowing your team members to bend or break rules and enable them to do their jobs better.

3. Hire enough sales support staff to handle the clerical/administrative stuff and free up your salespeople to *sell.*

4. Don't micromanage your team members—meaning, don't tell them *how* to do an action or second-guess them.

5. Provide constructive feedback to support team members' confidence: praise them in public and in private, but criticize only in private.

．
．
．

CHAPTER TWENTY-TWO

SHOWING THEM HOW TO MAKE
A DIFFERENCE TO THEIR CUSTOMERS

Throughout this book—especially in Chapters Two and Sixteen—I empha-
sized how charity and community can be a motivating force for Millennials. In Chapter Twenty, I suggested that you help provide *purpose* for
your team, which might have a charitable and/or community aspect
to it. The intertwining thread among all these ideas is that Millennials
are seeking to *make a difference* in some way through the combination
of work and play.

With the above in mind, I'm now going to show you how to help
your team members feel that they are making a difference without
the charity and community aspects—or even specifically addressing
purpose (which should always be there, in any case, to emotionally connect them to the business).

How? By showing them they can make the greatest difference by
serving the needs of the customer. In your training sessions, team meetings, and 1:1's with direct reports, propose to your team that they
avoid the word "sell" or "order" wherever possible with their buyers.
Internally, of course, it's all about "closing that sale" and "making the
numbers," but when meeting with customers the verbiage should re-
volve around concepts such as how you can . . .

- Help them solve a problem.
- Fill a need or want.
- Make them look good.
- Be responsive and available when they need you.
- Partner with them on their profit and growth.
- Maintain their trust.

With the above in mind, there are common phrases your team can apply:

- How may I be of service (or of help) to you? (Note: This is less effective in retail-sales scenarios, in which case you can just start with "Have you been to the store before?")
- How may I make things easier (or better) for you?
- Is there anything *I* can do better?

I'm not a huge fan of the phrase "relationship-building," because it's over-used and doesn't say much of anything. Your reps have "great relationships" with your buyers. That sounds nice (and maybe even implies that they're all dating each other). But so what? However, if they're *serving their customers* and *making a difference* to them, then they have established deep, meaningful connections that lead to trust and purchases.

The first step is for your reps to find out what their customers *actually do at their jobs.* I don't mean a job description, but rather a play-by-play of what fills their days—from the mundane and menial to the strategic and complicated. I guarantee that once the buyers get started explaining their activities, they will mention their *pain points.* This is where the reps demonstrate active listening (see Chapter Four) and repeat back what they've heard. This shows the buyers that *they heard what was said* and that *they care.* As an upside, it also helps the reps soak in the information for later use when the product or service is being pitched. When the customers lay their problems out on the table, it enables the reps to connect them to your offerings and emphasize that the benefits will help *solve their problems.*

A lot of reps are great at palling around with their buyers: lunches, coffees, drinks after work, social events (ballgames, concerts, etc.) These are opportunities for learning about more pain points—not just at work, but also in their personal lives. For example, the buyer might be a caregiver for a father with a terminal disease. Or perhaps confides that she has an autistic child. Your rep needs to pay attention to the details for the next e-mail, phone conversation, or in-person meeting. It may not be the first thing asked, but it could be the second or third. In a soft, empathic voice when others aren't around—you don't know if the buyer shared the information with anyone else—she can ask "How is your dad doing?" or "How is your son Matthew doing at school?" Then it's a matter of *listening*.

Making a difference with the buyer means celebrating the good times as well as the bad. Yeah, yeah, yeah—send the holiday cards and chocolate. However, it's far more important to send flowers to the buyer if her dad has passed away or if she's recovering from surgery. By the same token, send the flowers when the buyer gets married or has a baby (works just as well for a male as a female). It may even be memorable to send something memorable and funny on April Fool's Day, Valentine's Day, St. Patrick's Day, July 4th, or Halloween—if the rep knows that the buyer is into one of those holidays. (Of course, nothing too personal, suggestive, or grotesque—solid judgment is always required.) A rep can sometimes pick up on clues to a buyer's interests just based on what she sees in plain sight around the buyer's office or on her desk.

There are other creative ways for your reps to *make a difference* with their customers. Suppose the customer has a new product idea or improvement to one of your existing products. Your rep should compliment her on it—even if it's a terrible idea or one that's impractical. If the rep does bring it back to your company and it's accepted, well, then—your rep would immediately call the buyer to specially thank her and give her a great deal on ordering it. Every time the rep sees the buyer after that, she'd give a shout-out about her contribution. If her boss is there, it becomes an even more meaningful source of pride.

A PUBLISHING SALES STORY

Okay, there's room for one publishing-specific story in this book. I heard a story about a publishing sales rep who met with her account buyer. She'd gotten to know him pretty well and had an opportunity during a pitch meeting to pick his brain about new book ideas: "What do you think would work?" The buyer proceeded to offer a hot book idea to the rep, spending an hour citing why it was a big trend, what he thought should be in the book, and so forth. The rep took meticulous notes and brought them back to the publisher, who became super-excited and contracted with an author to write it.

A few months later, the same rep met with the same buyer and pitched him that book concept. "Nah . . . it won't sell. *Skip!*" he dismissed. Instead of getting flummoxed, the rep pulled out her notes from the previous meeting and recounted their conversation. She also showed him the acknowledgments in the book in which the author profusely thanked the buyer for having come up with the brilliant idea in the first place.

"Oh, right—*now* I remember!" the buyer recalled. "I'll take 5,000 copies and put it on a table for promotion."

The customer has been served.

The end result of all these caring activities is that your Millennial sales rep is finding fulfillment because she feels like she has *helped the customer*. She's made a meaningful difference, even if it's simply from paying attention and responding with empathy and support. When she sees that these efforts have led to sales, be sure to tell her that she has made a significant contribution and difference to *your* company because she has served and managed her account so well.

Things to Remember

1. Always strive to help your reps feel like they are making a difference with their customers.

2. Your reps can serve their customers by finding out what they do on any given day, uncovering their pain points, and connecting your product or service with the solutions to those problems.

3. Your reps need to pay attention to their customers at all times and remember everything they say—including details of their personal lives.

4. Reps should always connect with their customers for both the happy occasions (e.g., birth of a child) and the tragic ones (e.g., death of a loved one).

5. If a customer gives your rep an idea for a product or service—or even just an improvement—make sure the rep appropriately acknowledges the contribution and thanks her for it.

●
●
●

CHAPTER TWENTY-THREE

ENCOURAGING THEM TO MAKE DEALS AND CLOSE FAST

If you've read my book *Closing Techniques (That Really Work), Fourth Edition*, you know that I don't buy into any selling methods that involve trickery, manipulation, or lying. Forget the "moral/ethics" issues of these approaches for a second and understand one thing: they don't always work, though some salespeople might swear by them. Not only that, as was mentioned in Chapter Eleven (in this book, not the "going out of business" kind), you lose the respect of your sales team—and they will never directly tell you so. They'll just start filling out online job applications on indeed.com and other sites.

But suppose you need deals closed *fast*. You need to make your revenue targets—*or else*. The quarter is closing. Senior management is breathing down your neck. You may feel that your job is on the line, unless you and your team come through with something *big*.

You look at your back bench of sales professionals to determine who can come through for you. Max is slouched in his chair, texting on his phone. Skyler has her headphones on and is rhythmically bouncing in her seat to the music while scrolling up and down on various blog posts. Matthew's chair is empty and you have no idea *where* he might be. You're pretty sure he said he'd be in the office today, but between his jostling flex schedule and volunteer work, you can't seem to remember.

Who is going to deliver sales for you in a pinch? *Ugh.*

Remember the formula I presented in Chapter Eight?

Appointments give you Prospects which give you Sales

Now is the time to work with your team to dive deep into the data and determine how you are doing with your ratio:

1. Which customers buy the most frequently?
2. Which customers generate the most revenue?
3. Which customers have been known to take appointments on short notice?
4. Which customers make deals quickly?

Each of your reps should be assigned, sorting out customers by the above four criteria. For now, they should place their other prospects—i.e., the smaller fish and the ones straddling the fence—to the side. Have them assign the minor customer issues and problems to sales assistants and the major ones to you. Grease the wheels to alleviate any bureaucracy and processes that might be in their way. By doing so, you are enabling them to play to their strengths—*data research*—and play down the things that bore and/or distract them (the grunge work and dealing with the complaints). They also have no excuse to avoid contributing to your effort right away.

Now give them each specific targets to make by whenever they're needed (i.e., month or quarter). If they don't know their numbers to reach the goal, it's unlikely they will ever get there.

GETTING THE QUICK ORDER FROM A FREQUENT CUSTOMER

If you have a good, reliable customer who buys from you regularly and pays bills on time without any hassles, there are techniques to teasing out more sales in a hurry—and also some pitfalls that risk screwing up a good thing if one isn't careful. You need that right balance of finesse and caution.

Here's what your reps should *not* do: go in for the kill and pitch a mammoth discount for a major purchase if it is ordered the same day. This sounds like a good idea on the surface, but sometimes what happens is that the buyer might (a) think he was rooked by you in the past by not offering the best possible deal, or (b) you have established a new discount benchmark for the future that will be expected from you every time moving forward. In the latter scenario, all you've done is move up an order he already would have placed a month later—and given him a bigger discount on top of that. In the end, your company might have made the month—but you've shortchanged the quarter and have lowered your margins.

Instead: when your reps call upon these accounts, have them start off by asking these favored customers what they *like about your products* and what they *don't* like. Also have them ask the customers what they *aren't* getting from you and would like to receive.

No matter how the customers answer, your reps have gained trust of the buyers and haven't come across as desperate and pushy for rushed orders. Instead, they should listen, take note, and repeat back the positives and negatives. They can potentially address and repair the negatives right away—and then also offer them more of what is working as well as something from the list of things your company has not yet been providing.

Toward the end of the conversation, your rep can promise to fix the problem that day as a top priority. The rep next presents a mutual understanding with a sense of urgency on *both sides*: "I'll tell you what: even though it costs us a bit more, I'll change up our carton sizes for you right when I hang up the phone to help you out. If you send me a purchase order for 1,000 units of the new widgets today, I'll give you our preferred customer pricing right off the bat and we'll ship them first thing Monday. You'll have them in your warehouse by Wednesday."

The Millennials on your team will likely appreciate the reciprocal approach with their buyers, preferring it to charging right out of the gate with a hard sell that would probably put off the buyers anyway.

Give them a specific marching instruction: "Go!" You've cleared their plates so they can pound the phones with outreach that has a better-than-average chance of leading to conversion and revenue on short notice. They should be making appointments only with their frequent customers who generate the most revenue, will meet on short notice, and make quick decisions.

The sales leader has now devised a great plan and armed the team. The navy has shipped out to the open sea and it should all be smooth sailing, right? Well . . . not necessarily. I've heard from sales leaders that they conveyed the urgency to make sales several times at meetings, in 1:1's, and then in e-mail. The team seemed fired up at first, but then Friday comes and the sales leader looks around the office and—*whoa!* Max is texting, Skyler is catching up on her blogs, and Matthew is once again AWOL. Your team has reverted right back to where they started.

I've heard endless frustration from sales leaders about this. They just throw up their hands, blame the Millennials, and let things play out. This is the point where I challenge the sales leader to toughen up and hold the team accountable—*before it's too late.* That Friday—when everyone is suffering from the malaise—call an impromptu meeting to have everyone provide progress updates. Send out an S.O.S. to Matthew via e-mail, text, phone, or even a smoke signal: he is required to join in on this critical team discussion, no matter where he might be.

Ask each team member to prepare as follows for the meeting:

- How many calls did you make?
- How many e-mails did you send?
- How many appointments did you arrange?
- How many sales have you made so far?
- Where do you see yourself landing in terms of reaching the goal?

What do you think happens before the meeting that Friday afternoon? An explosive whirlwind of activity slams through your office. Everyone comes to life. Matthew miraculously flies through the front door and barrels into his seat. Phone calls are made, e-mails are sent, appointments are made, purchase orders are processed, calculators are whipped out. . . .

The meeting happens, and everyone is on his or her game, ready for you with the requested information. The numbers thus far are less than target—but, frankly, much better than what you initially expected.

What do you think made the difference? You—as mommy, daddy, or both—checked up on the children and held them accountable as responsible adults. They may have moaned or groaned at first but, deep down they craved the attention and needed your reassurance to continue to *Go!* Some of them might have experienced some customer declines out of the gate and felt discouraged. But by hearing the success stories of others at the meeting, they became encouraged and happily pressed on.

This "check-in" moment is a good opportunity to thank them for their collective efforts and to praise their hard work (even if it strikes you as having happened at the last minute). As mentioned many times in this book, appreciation and recognition are essential to Millennials.

Mainly, though, this is the right time to do a temperature take and see how team members are doing—and to show how much you care about their success. You are involved and invested in their efforts; you haven't thrown them in the deepest part of the ocean among the sharks without a float. You are all in it together and can help each other reach the target goal. There could be real reasons why some customers aren't biting on short notice: perhaps they are away on business or vacation; maybe they recently purchased from you and don't need any more of your product at the moment; or maybe there has been a shakeup in their company (such as a merger or acquisition) and all purchasing has been frozen.

The reps can't take any of these challenges to heart, and you need to help them: they need to remain motivated. Their adrenaline should be shooting through their veins as they make their way to closing deals.

This meeting also lets you add up the team's math and do a gap analysis to check on their pace and see how far they have to go. If you are falling well short in your percentages, then you need to go back to the formula with them: if necessary, widen the number of cold calls and e-mails to improve the amount of appointments and conversions.

It's never fun or easy when the heat is on and the sales need to happen on a dime. The one thing you can't do as sales leader is let up on driving your team out of fear that you are applying "too much pressure" to them and they might bolt at the next opportunity. Always be attuned to how team members are progressing, and keep them focused on their targets before the gap widens too far beyond anyone's reach and there is no time left to close it.

5 Things to Remember

1. When you need to close sales fast, target the customers who buy most frequently, generate the most revenue, take short-notice appointments, and make deals quickly.
2. Clear as many menial tasks as you can off your team's plate, so they can focus on bringing in maximum orders when you need them.
3. When approaching a frequent customer, the rep should never start off with "the big pitch," but rather ask if he has any issues with your products. After that, the rep can solve the problem that same day while offering other products for immediate shipping that fill their other needs or wants.
4. Set up a follow-up "check-in" meeting with your team at the end of the week to see how everyone is progressing toward achieving the target.
5. At the check-in meeting, praise their efforts while having them carefully examine their metrics to identify what is working and what is not; this will help guide the team on how to close the sales gap.

CHAPTER TWENTY-FOUR

ENSURING THAT THEY FEEL APPRECIATED, RESPECTED, AND VALUED

You may remember a time when a workforce stayed with a company for ten, fifteen, twenty, or even *thirty* years. The goal was to work long and hard, be loyal, and keep your head down so you could get a good bonus each year, earn a retirement pension, and maybe even receive a gold watch at a retirement party.

Well, we know that is no longer the case. The stereotype is that Millennials have one foot out the door; not only are they changing jobs every one to three years, they are changing *career paths* with regularity as well. From everything I've seen and heard, Millennials are not choosing to stay in *sales jobs* for very long.

These are the main retention issues—all of which have been covered in earlier chapters in one way or another but bear repeating:

1. They don't see a career path and aren't being promoted as quickly as they feel they deserve.
2. They don't feel a connection or sense of *purpose* with their company.
3. They don't feel they receive enough recognition for their work and accomplishments.
4. They are put off by the company's bureaucracy and/or hierarchy.
5. They don't feel they are being given the opportunity to contribute enough to the company—or to a greater cause.

Compared to other organizational departments, sales is an outlier in terms of necessary skillset and mindset. Salespeople need to have enormous confidence, be aggressive, withstand a lot of rejection (and overcome it), *and* be able to finesse and retain relationships. If any one or a combination of the above five retention issues is a problem for a young sales rep, she will be out the door before you can say *Og Mandino* (author of the old classic book *The Greatest Salesman in the World*).

A salesperson used to be motivated by a paycheck, a bonus check, and the occasional pat on the back. They basked in the limelight when they won "salesman of the year" awards. I don't see nearly as much of this going on in the workplace anymore, probably because it's become passé.

Even so, you need to find ways to retain good people and keep them happy and motivated. So, what really works? Of course, it's right in the title of this chapter: being *appreciated, respected,* and *valued.* But what do these three things really look like? What can a sales leader *do*?

Here's the secret*: embed appreciation in your department's culture.* Don't wait until someone "saves the day" with a monster sale to offer recognition and thanks. It needs to be a possibility *at any time.*

I've heard various statistics on how often Millennials need to receive some tangible form of appreciation. It's somewhere between once a week and once a month. My suggestion is to at least try to make it happen two or three times a month.

How do you embed this in the culture without it coming across as forced? The first scenario is obvious: showing *appreciation* for people who stay by recognizing work anniversaries. You may be asking: "So what?" How is that an accomplishment? Let me tell you: it seems like a little thing, but it means a lot to your team members and enables them to see that you are *paying attention* and actually *want them to stay.* It also shows that dedication, loyalty, and years of service actually *do* matter to you and your organization.

Keep tabs on work anniversaries for all your team members— whether it's one year or ten—and do a shout-out at every meeting: "Jasmine is celebrating her one-year anniversary today—congratulations, Jasmine!"

Don't stop there. Send Jasmine an e-card. Serve her favorite snack at the meeting. (If you don't know what that is, chances are you don't know her as well as you should.) Buy her a $10 Starbucks card or a ticket to a concert or other event.

I've actually heard some bosses worry about the expense of these things spread out across an entire sales force. They don't "have the budget" for it. I say *"You've got to be freaking kidding me!"* Suppose you have ten people on your team; that's ten anniversaries at $10 a pop. It's not worth *$100* or less than ten bucks a month to avoid turnover? How much does it cost in job ads, recruiting fees, and training new employees? How much does it cost you in lost time and unmet sales due to unfulfilled positions during transitions—not to mention the intangibles, such as customer relationships and institutional knowledge about your company's products and services? When it comes to retaining your sales stars, don't ever think small or cheap.

Of course, not every token of gratitude needs to cost something. Sometimes a handwritten card has more meaning than an e-card, even to a technology-driven Millennial.

There is an art to the verbal display of appreciation. You can't simply praise or thank an employee for a "good job" at a meeting. If you multiply that out by ten employees on repeated occasions, it starts to sound stale and repetitive.

Be creative and mix up the scenarios. Offer the praise or thank-you at an *unexpected* moment, not during your standing department meeting. It could be at a company meeting, during a group session with other departments, or even just when passing the rep in the hallway. Whatever you do, *don't wait too long!* If a week goes by before you offer praise to an employee, the moment slips away and it becomes old news.

THE "PAT ON THE BACK"—21ST-CENTURY STYLE ★

If you want to offer spontaneous praise to your rep, a shout-out or pat on the back in the hallway is *"meh."* You could do better and kick it up a notch to provide greater meaning. No matter what else is going on or who you or the rep might be with, stop him in the hallway and say "Hey, Connor—hold on a second." Turn to him in slow motion, look him right in the eye, and state "I like how you handled closing the deal with Acme yesterday. It was a tough sell, but you came through with the exact right questions—and provided some strong solutions with our products. Thanks—and keep it up!" I guarantee your message will stick and he'll feel good about it: Connor will go home that night and tell his friends and family about what you said to him.

Notice in the above that the gratitude expresses positive reinforcement not just for closing the sale, but also for asking the *right questions* and for providing *strong solutions*. Take the opportunity to emphasize the technique *that worked* to give the rep confidence for the next appointment. It also helps other people within earshot understand what it takes to find success and get that 21st-century pat on the back.

If you really want employees to feel that they are valued, offer praise to them in front of other department heads and senior executives. Or, if you are in a meeting with an important buyer, praise your rep right there and then. This serves many purposes, in addition to making the rep blush and feel recognized: it shows your customer that you appreciate and support your team; and it boosts the customer's confidence that you have a top person handling the account.

Another effective way to do this is to have *another colleague* pass along the praise directly. Again, if it comes from you, the rep may just hear the Charlie Brown adult saying "*wah-wah-wah.*" But, if it comes from a fellow rep, a different department head, or an executive, it will be truly meaningful. It doesn't need to be as specific as praise coming from you. The CEO could simply say, "Hey, Connor, I heard from Steve, your supervisor, that you nailed the Acme account. Whatever you did, keep doing it. Great job!"

It goes without saying that, if one of your customers offers a compliment about one of your reps, read the e-mail at a department meeting—or even in front of the company. There is nothing better than receiving praise from outside your organization that is recognized within.

I know I'm beating this to death, but I can't over-stress the importance of *appreciation, respect,* and *being valued.* If one person feels disrespected in any fashion, I can guarantee that that person is talking to a colleague and planting some doubt about the company in her brain.

Lastly: however and whenever you offer a compliment to a rep in front of a group, try to *tell a story about it.* Don't just say, "Thanks to Brittany for closing the Acme account—great job!" It will fall flat and won't ring true. The details actually do matter. Stories convey emotion and demonstrate that you are paying attention. The more specific you can be in your storytelling, the more impact and meaning it will have. I'll close this chapter with an example I recently heard:

> As some of you know, Samantha just came back from her trip to India. I don't know if you are aware of what happened, but . . . her flight out on Tuesday was delayed eight hours and then finally canceled at 2:00 a.m. She stayed at a fleabag motel from 3:00 a.m. to 5:00 a.m. and then got back to the airport for the first flight out. That flight was canceled. She managed to get on another flight that afternoon—but it had three connections. The first landing was too late to make the second connection, so she took a different flight that missed her third connection. She finally made it, a full day and a half late into Indira Gandhi Airport . . . and guess what: they lost her bags! Somehow Samantha bought some clothes, made it to her hotel, cleaned up, and made it to the meeting with the buyer—just before he was about to give up and cancel. Despite a limited amount of time, several objections, and competitive pricing, Samantha was able to close the deal by offering their team some of our empty office space for use at no charge when they come to town. I don't know if I would have thought of something so clever on the spot—especially without having slept in over a day!

Things to Remember

1. Salespeople will not remain with a company for long if they don't feel *appreciated* on a regular basis.
2. Embed *appreciation* in your department culture by celebrating work anniversaries—whether it's the first year or twentieth.
3. Showing appreciation doesn't require spending a lot of money: a $10 gift card or even a handwritten note will suffice.
4. Be spontaneous with compliments—mix up the *how, when,* and *where* and do not play favorites among team members.
5. When showing gratitude, try to tell a story about the employee's accomplishment, as it demonstrates authenticity.

CHAPTER TWENTY-FIVE

:
:

PROVIDING NEW OPPORTUNITIES AND FUTURE CHALLENGES

While your number-one thought is on how you and your team will achieve your sales targets, your direct reports are focusing on their respective futures in the organization. They want to find *purpose* in what they do and want to know what roles they can look forward to filling down the line. As I've stated many times in this book, they are also extremely impatient and may jump ship if they don't feel that their needs, wants, and ambitions are being fulfilled soon enough in your company.

You may think such ambition makes them feel "entitled." Whether this is the case or not shouldn't matter to you as the sales leader. You need to give your team enough training, regular feedback, motivation, recognition, and job freedom so they feel comfortable and confident and *sell, sell, sell.*

Along the way, you also need to figure out what makes each person *tick.* As you are providing team *purpose,* you also need to sit down with each team member—at least those performing at a satisfactory level or better—and have a conversation in which you ask the following questions:

1. What tasks do you *like* about your job?
2. What tasks do you *dislike* about your job?
3. What do you see yourself doing in five years?
4. What can I do to make your job better or easier?
5. Do you feel like you are being challenged enough?
6. What is something you *aren't* doing now that you'd like to try?

Some employees will sit there dumbfounded and answer "I dunno" to every question. Others will spend a half hour answering each question, if you let them. The main thing you need answered is what you can do to help provide *fulfillment* for them. Instead of driving the process, you are empowering them to create their own paths.

If someone wants to transfer from Sales into Marketing (or some other department), that can be okay too, even though it sets you back a valued team member should that situation occur. Do everything you can to help an employee get to where he or she wants to go within the organization. By providing the tools, skills, openings, and encouragement to move up and around, you are still providing a service to the organization by helping company retention efforts. In the end, this will pay off for you because the employee who shifted to Marketing will see both you and the company in a positive light, and may recommend other people she knows to fill vacant sales positions.

Millennials are hungry to learn and will appreciate anything you suggest that will help them get closer to their long-term goals—as long as the individual and company goals are being met and the employee's performance at least meets company standards. During your 1:1's discuss these options:

1. **Supplemental online training:** This could be in sales or on topics in other areas, such as marketing.

2. **Workshops, conferences, seminars, and lectures:** Again, these don't need to be 100% connected to sales.

3. **Adult education:** Many companies offer tuition reimbursement. If this is the case, find out the employee's areas of interest and make suggestions on what courses might be applicable.

4. **Stretch goals:** Assign a project that is a step above the employee's skill set and experience. She'll appreciate the chance to succeed and prove herself.

5. **Shifting accounts:** If a rising star employee is "stuck" handling a certain type of account and wants a greater challenge, find a way to empower her with a customer who is higher stakes (and probably much more demanding).

In all the above scenarios, you want the employee to "own" the responsibility and fill you in on how these developmental activities are working for her. Encourage her to share some of her big-picture takeaways with the team, especially with regard to anything of note from the online training and adult education. It could be as simple as sharing untapped networks for sales leads, a few pointers on getting spreadsheets done faster, or new apps from Salesforce.com. Sometimes just describing the experience of meeting certain people at these events or gathering competitive intel while in attendance creates shared team engagement and encourages other team members to take advantage of development opportunities themselves.

Most of all, find out if the developmental tasks are connecting in terms of helping her with her current job and long-term goals. If they aren't, that's okay. Don't make it seem like it was a waste of time or money. Never judge these activities: what you see as irrelevant (and vice versa) may not seem the same to your sales rep.

OPPORTUNITIES MATERIALIZE WHEN THEY JUST SHOW UP

Jennifer was an up-and-coming star rep for a biotech company. Out of nowhere, she hit a rough patch and things came to a screeching halt for her. She thought she had lost her touch. Her biggest prospect, George Brimbly, whom she had never met face to face, had fallen off the map and stopped returning her calls and e-mails. This had never happened to her before, and she didn't know what to do.

When she met with Donna, her boss, at their weekly 1:1, Jennifer was surprised that they didn't discuss her sales drought at all. In fact, they talked about Jennifer's future ambitions, long-term goals, and side interests. It turned out that she was interested in learning about public speaking. While she'd already done many sales pitches, she'd never spoken to a large group.

Donna lit up with excitement as she described how the company helped subsidize memberships with Toastmasters International. By good fortune, it happened that there was an upcoming event she thought might be of interest to her.

Jennifer leaped at the opportunity. She attended the event and soaked everything in. By sheer coincidence, George Brimbly was on one of the panels at the event! During a break, she marched over to him and introduced herself with an extended hand and a professional, winning smile.

"*You* are Jennifer?" he reacted with some embarrassment. "I'm so sorry. I received all your messages and e-mails. I feel terrible about not having gotten back to you. I was traveling and then got really backed up. I thought I was too late and had missed the boat. Can I still place my order at the same price?"

The story had the happy ending you'd hope for: Jennifer closed the deal and ultimately became an excellent public speaker, to boot.

In any case, whether a developmental opportunity is a success or failure, always be receptive to the next one—if your schedules and goals allow it. Keep on the lookout for things that might be of interest to your employees for growth, not just "areas of improvement." If you focus too much on the latter, your employee may view you as a micromanaging dictator and feel like you're taking all the fun out of it. It's kind of like you were a kid and your parents signed you up for more piano lessons, despite the fact that you exclaimed, "I suck at it, I hate it, and I never want to play the piano again!"

"Maybe if you had more lessons and practiced more, you'd like it better," your (rather dense) parent responds (in the "*wah-wah-wah*" adult Charlie Brown voice, of course).

Suddenly, *development* becomes *punishment*. Be certain you always distinguish between development activities that are for personal and professional growth, not a requirement for improving tasks to meet company standards (which are extremely important but separate).

As mentioned, it's fine to ask the employee to share the things she's learned with the group and even write up a summary, but make sure she doesn't turn the latter into a term paper, either. The task is to memorialize the high points, not assign hours of unnecessary homework that takes away from selling.

5 **Things to Remember**

1. Make time in your schedule with your direct reports who are meeting or exceeding expectations to share long-term personal and professional goals; this will help shape a development plan.

2. Encourage and facilitate growth areas—even those that might be outside an employee's job responsibilities.

3. Avoid judging the outcomes of an outside training session attended by an employee.

4. Separate out *development* opportunities from activities intended to resolve *areas of improvement.*

5. Empower your employee to share her findings from a recent development activity, but don't pile on excessive summary-report writing, either.

CONCLUSION

In my book *The 25 Habits of Highly Successful Salespeople,* I wrote: "The successful salesperson makes a good leader because he or she inspires trust."

That book has been around for many years in multiple editions that predate the Millennial generation (and I admit, I certainly did *not* see them coming!), but those quoted words hold true today more than ever. If there is a binding theme among the twenty-five chapters in this book, it's the word *trust.*

As a salesperson, you must earn the *trust* of your customers. As a sales leader, you need to earn the *trust* of your Millennial team members. If you had asked me about this a couple of decades ago, I probably would have said it was the exact opposite way around—your employees need to earn *your* trust. But times change, and one would be foolish to try to manage people the same way year after year.

If you earn your team's trust, offer frequent constructive feedback, make work fun, create a career path, and give them space to do "*their thing* on *their schedule* and without *negatively impacting sales and inconveniencing customers and coworkers,*" you will retain your valued team members and establish a back bench of talented people who are proud to work for you and stay with your company. In time, you'll gain an appreciation for their different styles and possibly even learn a thing or two from them as well (or at least all the latest slang terms and emojis).

Wherever your sales reps end up in the long run, your encouragement and support are what they will remember about you and your company. So, even if they do ultimately abandon ship for other horizons, they may someday reappear in your circle and refer business to you, recommend a new hire, or even help you find a job in the unlikely event something goes south with your current position.

Who knows? One of these Millennials may be *your boss* someday.

Would that really be so bad? If that happens, don't scratch your head and shout out that the universe is unfair and has no meaning.

Instead, be proud: you will have created a *sales star*.

REFERENCES

INTRODUCTION

Adkins, Amy. "Millennials: The Job-Hopping Generation," May 12, 2016. https://news.gallup.com/businessjournal/191459/millennials-job-hopping-generation.aspx

Fry, Richard. "Millennials Are the Largest Generation in the U.S. Labor Force," April 11, 2018. http://www.pewresearch.org/fact-tank/2018/04/11/millennials-largest-generation-us-labor-force/

CHAPTER 1

Zenger, Jack and Folkman, Joseph. "What Great Listeners Actually Do," July 14, 2016. https://hbr.org/2016/07/what-great-listeners-actually-do

CHAPTER 8

Schiffman, Stephan. http://www.steveschiffman.com/videos/

Schiffman, Stephan. *Cold Calling Techniques (That Really Work), Seventh Edition*, Adams Media, 2013.

Disney, Daniel. "Millennials Will End Cold Calling By 2025," November 29, 2017. https://thedailysales.net/millennials-will-end-cold-calling-by-2025/

Hoos, Aaron. "Business Lessons from *Planes, Trains and Automobiles*," November 29, 2009. https://aaronhoos.com/2009/11/26/business-lessons-from-planes-trains-and-automobiles/

CHAPTER 10

Jenkins, Ryan. "This Is Why Millennials Care so Much About Work-Life Balance," https://www.inc.com/ryan-jenkins/this-is-what-millennials-value-most-in-a-job-why.html

Rampton, John. "9 Harsh Realities of What Motivates Millennial Workers," https://www.inc.com/john-rampton/9-harsh-realities-of-what-motivates-millennial-wor.html

CHAPTER 12

Pelletier, Sue. "9 Effective Ways to Engage Millennials at Your Events," May 14, 2017. http://www.meetingsnet.com/event-design-ideas/9-effective-ways-engage-millennials-your-events

CHAPTER 13

Borrelli, David. "There's a Reason Millennials Want a Culture of Collaboration at Work," December 12, 2014.

Kang, Erin. "5 Reasons Millennials Hate Meetings—and How to Engage Them," July 1, 2015. http://www.successfulmeetings.com/Strategy/Meeting-Strategies/5-Reasons-Millennials-Hate-Meetings--and-How-to-Engage-Them/

CHAPTER 15

Schiffman, Stephan. *25 Toughest Sales Objections (and How to Overcome Them)*, McGraw-Hill, 2011.

CHAPTER 16

Brooks, Jeb. "The World's Most Complete List of Job Titles for Salespeople." https://brooksgroup.com/sales-training-blog/worlds-most-complete-list-job-titles-salespeople-0

CHAPTER 17
https://emojipedia.org/food-drink/

CHAPTER 18
Kelly, Douglas. "Millennials Want Workplace Ethics and Diversity," April 12, 2017. http://blog.lawroom.com/ethical-conduct/millennials-want-workplace-ethics-diversity/

Field, Anne. "Millennials Want Companies Mixing Mission And Money" December 11, 2017. https://www.forbes.com/sites/annefield/2017/12/11/millennials-want-companies-mixing-mission-and-money/#25b48873bf2c

Pelosi, Peggie. "Millennials Want Workplaces With Social Purpose. How Does Your Company Measure Up?" February 20, 2018. http://www.talenteconomy.io/2018/02/20/millennials-want-workplaces-social-purpose-company-measure/

CHAPTER 19
Wigo, Lindsay. "Most Millennials Approve of Tattoos, Piercings, but Affects Job Hiring," March 15, 2017. http://desalesminstrel.org/2017/03/15/most-millennials-approve-of-tattoos-piercings-but-affects-job-hiring/

Jenkins, Ryan. "How to Attract and Retain Millennials With the Right Dress Code," https://www.inc.com/ryan-jenkins/how-to-attract-and-retain-millennials-with-the-right-dress-code.html

CHAPTER 20
Miles, Bryan. "Purpose Driven Millennials: How to Attract and Engage Gen Y," April 2, 2018. https://www.thebalancecareers.com/engaging-millennial-workforce-4045064

CHAPTER 22
Hysen, Britt. "Millennials Making a Social Impact," December 6, 2017. https://www.huffingtonpost.com/britt-hysen/millennials-making-a-soci_b_5851186.html

CHAPTER 23
Schiffman, Stephan. *Closing Techniques (That Really Work)*, Adams Media, 2009.

CHAPTER 24
Sturt, David. "Here's How Often Millennial Employees Need Compliments," February 8, 2017. http://fortune.com/2017/02/07/how-to-manage-a-millennial/

CHAPTER 25
Adkins, Amy and Rigonia, Brandon. "Millennials Want Jobs to Be Development Opportunities," *Gallup Business Journal*, June 30, 2016. https://news.gallup.com/businessjournal/193274/millennials-jobs-development-opportunities.aspx

CONCLUSION
Schiffman, Stephan. *The 25 Habits of Highly Successful Salespeople, 3rd Edition*, May 2008.

INDEX